Questions of the Spirit

A Collection of Answers

Michelle E. Keith

with Tim Quinn

Published by Michelle Keith and Tim Quinn

Other titles from these authors include:

In the Arena: Building the Skills for Peak Performance in Leading Schools and Systems
The Superintendent Search Process: A Guide to Getting the Job and Getting Off to a Great Start
Peak Performing Governance Teams: Creating an Effective Board/Superintendent Partnership
Within Reach: Leadership Lessons in School Reform from Charlotte-Mecklenburg Schools
Tales from the Top: Stories Only School Superintendents Could Tell
The Old Mission Cook: Recipes for Using and Preserving Our Local Produce

All profits from the sale of this book are dedicated to scholarship programs for high needs youth.

ISBN: 9798353833987

Independently Published

Table of Contents

Introduction

The older I get, the more obvious it becomes that I don't have all of life's answers. In fact, I'm not even sure I am asking the right questions! But, again, in getting older, you naturally start to think about your life, asking yourself what has it all meant? Where is it going? What do I still believe? What do I still need to do?

For years, I have gathered quotes, poems, and other writings that have inspired me, made me think, provided a new perspective on a spiritual question, or even disturbed my way of thinking. They've been stuck in drawers, marked by dog-ears in books, saved electronically, or committed to memory. Being the kind of person who doesn't like messes, it was past time to organize and pull them together in a way that makes some sense, so I can more easily find the nuggets when I need them.

We have self-published a few other books, so I decided to use that format for this project. In making it more useful for me, it also makes the thoughts more easily shareable, in case others are asking similar questions.

What is in the book are a few of life's big questions, along with the ideas, quotes, or poems I have collected that provide some perspectives on the possible answers that seem to make some sense to me.

While I've tried to correctly attribute each author quoted and included a bibliography at the end, the book is not heavily footnoted. The book is <u>not</u> a scholarly examination of life's universal questions, presenting and evaluating all sides of an issue. It's not an exhaustive look into all the numerous religions of the world.

I was raised a Christian, so I'm naturally grounded in that perspective of life. I don't apologize for that. People with other upbringings will start from different reference points. (They can put together their own books and perhaps we'll learn from each other!)

Spiritual matters are deeply personal. Some of the quotes and ideas may differ from your beliefs, and that's OK. It's not a criticism of other ways of thinking; I'm simply sharing thoughts and ideas that make sense to <u>me</u> – but may not make any sense at all to others.

In *The Road Less Traveled,* M. Scott Peck wrote:

> "One of our problems is that very few of us have developed any distinctive personal life. Everything about us seems secondhand, even our emotions. In many cases we have to rely on secondhand information in order to function. I accept the word of a physician, a scientist, a farmer, on trust. I do not like to do this. I have to because they possess vital knowledge of living of which I am ignorant. Secondhand information concerning the state of my kidneys, the effects of cholesterol, and the raising of chickens, I can live with. But when it comes to questions of meaning, purpose, and death, secondhand information will not do. I cannot survive on a secondhand faith in a secondhand God. There has to be a personal word, a unique confrontation, if I am to come alive."

So, what we have are questions that we each need to try to answer in our own way, in a way that makes sense in our own unique life.

Deepak Chopra wrote, *"Walk with those who are looking for the truth, run from those who think they have found it."*

I know I still don't have all the answers and will continue to revisit the questions. And I'll still collect new quotes and poems, because people smarter and more articulate than I will continue to say smart things in an articulate way.

Writer and theologian Frederick Beuchner wrote:

> *"Faith is a journey without maps. Faith is not being sure where you are going, but going anyway. We must be willing to walk in the paradox of life's uncertainties; to be content with living the questions without having to know all the answers."*

I hope you, also, find some ideas of value for your life in these thoughts.

Chapter 1

How Can I Find Peace in a Troubled World?

How can I possibly be happy and still have hope when I wake up in the morning, look at my news feed, and am bombarded with:

- Mass shootings
- Natural disasters, fueled by climate change
- Wars, poverty, and hunger
- Racism, bigotry, and hatred
- People attacking each other and spreading lies on social media
- Extremists on the right and on the left, unwilling to see that truth and good solutions are often in the middle
- Elected officials unwilling or unable to do anything about any of the above
- People continuing to elect those officials
- And on and on and on.

Some days it seems like making the choice to be happy is naïve and the equivalent of just living with my head in the sand. Has there always been this much bad news? (After all, the phrase "going to hell in a handbasket" originated sometime during the 18th century, when the heads of guillotine victims were captured in baskets.) Does it just seem worse now that it's at our fingertips 24/7? Or, am I just noticing it more because I'm retired and don't have other business to fill my head?

I can't live my days being angry, fearful, and upset. How can I stay positive in the face of all this? How can I avoid contributing to the hate and anger in the world?

Here are some brief thoughts and longer essays that others have shared on this topic that help me live most days on an even keel.

Caroline Myss, an author and speaker on human consciousness, as quoted in the book The Wisdom of Sundays says:

"Your spirit is the part of you that is seeking meaning and purpose... Another way to understand spirit is that it's the part of you that is drawn to hope, that will not give in to despair. The part of you that has to believe in goodness; that has to believe in something more."

From Rumi, the 13th century Persian poet, Islamic scholar and mystic (Mathnawi VI, 3280-3287):

Why Be Cruel to Yourself

Your grace is the shepherd of all who have been created,
guarding them from the wolf of pain—
a loving shepherd like God's pen, Moses.
A single sheep fled from him: Moses wore out his shoes
and his feet blistered as he followed after it.
He continued searching until night fell;
meanwhile the flock had vanished from sight.
The lost sheep was weak and exhausted;
Moses shook the dust from it
and stroked its back and head with his hand,
fondling it lovingly like a mother.
Not a bit of irritation and anger,
nothing but love and pity and tears!
He said to the sheep, "I can understand

That you naturally had no pity on me,
but why did your nature show such cruelty to itself?"

■■

From Parker Palmer, author and educator who focused on leadership and spirituality:

"A community *always* includes the people we wish would go away."

■■

My partner, Tim Quinn, has observed:

"If it bleeds, it leads. Today's media (television, radio, news outlets, social media) know that fear and anger can be monetized in a big way. They depend on ad income, which is driven by viewership. Bad news and controversy sell, and therefore increase viewership. That is why on a 30-minute newscast, you'll be fed 27 minutes of bad news, ending with a 3-minute happy segment."

■■

A study published in Harvard Business Review, by Arianna Huffington, Michelle Gielan, and Shawn Achor, showed that being exposed to three minutes of negative news results in a 27% higher chance of having a bad day. Great!

But there's help. RadicalTransformationProject.com, tells how to manage your news consumption and remain sane:

1. Consume news in small doses. Don't consume news all day long. Pick one time of the day to check in on what's happening in the world and stick to it.

2. Pick a focus. It's impossible to follow/care about everything. What is it you care about most? Focus on that area and skim others, and you won't feel so powerless or helpless.
3. Be critical. Critically analyze what you read/hear. Realize a lot of media is coming from a place of bias. Search for the least biased sources for world, national, state and local news. Distinguish *news* from *opinion*. Read sources you disagree with. Challenge yourself by trying to understand all the different points of view on an issue.
4. Detox regularly. Don't consume any news for a day, a weekend.
5. Do something. Pick *one* cause to get personally involved in and let others work on other issues.

A good reminder from children's book author Lemony Snicket:

"It is very unnerving to be proven wrong, particularly when you are really right and the person who is really wrong is proving you wrong and proving himself, wrongly, right."

From that great source "Anonymous":

The best criticism of the bad is practice of the better.

When we judge or criticize another person, it says nothing about that person; it merely says something about our own need to be critical.

Yoko Ono (artist and wife of the late John Lennon):

"Try to say nothing negative about anybody for three days, for forty-five days, for three months. See what happens to your life."

In The Wisdom of Sundays, Oprah Winfrey wrote:

"There was a time when I believed the act of forgiveness meant accepting the offender, and by doing so, condoning the act. I didn't understand that the true purpose of forgiveness is to stop allowing whatever that person did to affect how I live my life now."

An excerpt from Long Walk to Freedom, Nelson Mandela's life story, reminds me that if Mandela didn't give up hope after 27 years in prison, what do I have to whine about?

"In another conversation I said, 'Tell me the truth. When you were leaving prison after twenty-seven years and walking down that road to freedom, didn't you hate them all over again?' And he said, 'Absolutely I did, because they'd imprisoned me for so long. I was abused. I didn't get to see my children grow up. I lost my marriage and the best years of my life. I was angry. And I was afraid, because I had not been free in so long. But as I got closer to the car that would take me away, I realized that when I went through that gate, if I still hated them, they would still have me. I wanted to be free. And so I let it go.'"

Mandela said, "I am fundamentally an optimist, whether that comes from nature or nurture, I cannot say. Part of being optimistic is keeping one's head pointed toward the sun, one's feet moving forward. There were many dark moments when my faith in humanity was sorely tested, but I would not and could not give myself up to despair. That way lays defeat and death."

Archbishop Helder Camara:

"When I give food to the poor, they call me a saint. When I ask why the poor have no food, they call me a socialist."

From author Anne Lamott:

"You can tell if people are following Jesus, because they are feeding the poor, sharing their wealth, and trying to get everyone medical insurance."

From Rumi (Mathnawi I, 3347-3348):

"A conceited person sees some sin,
And the flames of Hell rise up in him.
He calls that hellish pride defense of the Religion;
He doesn't notice his own arrogant soul."

Deepak Chopra, Indian-American author and alternative medicine advocate offers good advice from his book The Seven Spiritual Laws of Success:

1) ***The law of pure potentiality***. All things are possible. Take time to be silent, commune with nature, and

practice non-judgment to get in touch with your consciousness.

2) ***The law of giving (and receiving)***. All relationships are a give and take. Bring a gift to whoever you encounter, receive all the gifts life has to offer, keep wealth circulating by giving and receiving life's gifts.
3) ***The law of "Karma" or cause & effect***. Every action generates a force of energy that returns to us in like kind. When we choose actions that bring happiness and success to others, the fruit of our karma is happiness and success. Witness the choices you make and ask yourself what the consequences are – if it will bring happiness and fulfillment.
4) ***The law of least effort***. Nature's intelligence functions with ease and carefreeness. Accept situations as they occur, take responsibility for what is happening, relinquish the need to defend your point of view.
5) ***The law of intention and desire***. When we introduce an intention into the pure field of pure potentiality, we put this infinite organizing power to work for us. Know your desires, release your attachment to the outcome, and enjoy the process and the journey.
6) ***The law of detachment***. Be willing to step into the uncertain, the unknown, surrender yourself to the creative.
7) ***The law of "Dharma" or purpose in life***. Everyone has a purpose in life...a unique gift or special talent to give to others. And when we blend this unique talent with service to others, we experience the ecstasy and exultation of our own spirit, which is the ultimate goal of all goals.

In 1963, the Rev. Dr. Martin Luther King, Jr. wrote an open letter to other leaders of the clergy:

Letter from Birmingham Jail (excerpt)

"I am coming to feel that the people of ill will have used time much more effectively than the people of good will. We will have to repent in this generation not merely for the vitriolic works and actions of the bad people, but for the appalling silence of the good people. We must come to see that human progress never rolls in on wheels of inevitability. It comes through the tireless efforts and persistent work of men willing to be co-workers with God, and without this hard work itself becomes an ally of the forces of social stagnation. We must use time creatively, and forever realize that the time is always ripe to do right."

From James 1:19-27 (New International Version):

"My dear brothers and sisters, take note of this: Everyone should be quick to listen, slow to speak and slow to become angry, because human anger does not produce the righteousness that God desires. Therefore, get rid of all moral filth and the evil that is so prevalent and humbly accept the word planted in you, which can save you.

"Do not merely listen to the word, and so deceive yourselves. Do what it says. Anyone who listens to the word but does not do what it says is like someone who looks at his face in a mirror and, after looking at himself, goes away and immediately forgets what he looks like. But whoever looks intently into the perfect law that gives freedom and continues in it – not forgetting what they have heard but doing it – they will be blessed in what they do. Those who consider themselves religious and yet do not keep a tight rein on their tongues deceive themselves, and their religion is worthless. Religion that God our Father accepts as pure and faultless is this: to look after orphans and widows in their distress and to keep oneself from being polluted by the world."

Richard Rohr is a Franciscan priest and writer who will be quoted often in this book. In his Daily Meditation on 1/28/15, he wrote:

From the beginning until now, the entire creation as we know it has been groaning in one great act of giving birth. —Romans 8:22

"Creation did not happen once by a flick of the Divine hand, and now it's slowly winding down – which is what we've assumed for most of history. Creation, in fact, is a process that is still happening and winding up, and even better, *we're in on it!* We are a part of this endless creativity of God. Talk about inclusion and how everything belongs! In other words, YOU matter and YOU make a difference!

"The reason this is so hard for us to see in our little, tiny moments of history, is that this groaning and this giving birth proceeds by a process of losses and gains, and the losses are very real. There is no doubt that history, like the biblical text itself, goes three steps forward and two steps back. Thank God, there always seems to be a net gain to history and to the biblical text too. Even though we see violence, war, genocide, and stupidity, and we see religions and factions circling the wagons around their own tiny identities, yet always it happens that something like Vatican II, Nelson Mandela, Mother Teresa, or Pope Francis comes out of seeming nowhere! Where does this high level, enlightened thinking come from?

"It seems history moves forward, and then we say, 'No, no, no! This is too much freedom; it's too scary.' So we pull back into denial and resistance (Joshua and Judges after Exodus, Napoleon after the French Revolution, Tridentine Masses after Vatican II). But the movement of history cannot be stopped. There is always a leaven that remains, a critical mass, a few people who get it, and the toothpaste is out of the tube forever. Once the toothpaste is out of the tube, you can't put it back in. You can't tell people they don't know once they know the Bigger Truth. So history proceeds, nevertheless, and the Second Coming of Christ is this ever new level of Christ-people that keeps emerging despite continual regression into 'passion and death,' exactly as revealed in the body of Jesus. I cannot wait to ask God why this seems to be the divine and chosen pattern of all true development and growth."

And a final thought from Rumi (Mathnawi V, 134;138-139):

Intelligence and Tears

Till the cloud weeps, how should the garden smile?
The weeping of the cloud and the burning of the sun
are the pillars of this world: twist these two strands together.
Since the searing heat of the sun and the moisture of the clouds
keep the world fresh and sweet,
keep the sun of your intelligence burning bright
and your eye glistening with tears.

Chapter Two

What Can I Do to Make a Difference?

There are so many problems in the world, and I feel I should be doing *something* to help make things better. But my "circle of influence" is so small (and getting smaller.) I'm not going to run for president – heck, I don't even want to run for office in my local township! So, I recycle, donate some money here and there, volunteer occasionally. But does any of that make any difference at all? What should my contribution be?

Here are some thoughts that help me reflect on my answer to this question.

■■

On his deathbed, St. Francis of Assisi told his brethren, "I have done what was mine to do; may Christ teach you what is yours."

(from St. Anthony Spiritual Center)

■■

To Be of Use, *by Marge Piercy (from the book Teaching with Fire)*

The people I love the best
jump into work head first
without dallying in the shallows
and swim off with sure strokes almost out of sight.
They seem to become natives of that element,
the black sleek heads of seals
bouncing like half-submerged balls.

I love people who harness themselves, an ox to a heavy cart,
who pull like water buffalo, with massive patience,
who strain in the mud and the muck to move things forward.,
who do what has to be done, again and again.

I want to be with people who submerge
in the task, who go into the fields to harvest
and work in a row and pass the bags along,
who are not parlor generals and field deserters
but who move in the common rhythm
when the food must come in or the fire be put out.

The work of the world is common as mud.
Botched, it smears the hands, crumbles to dust.
But the thing worth doing well done
has a shape that satisfies, clean and evident.
Greek amphoras for wine or oil,
Hopi vases that held corn, are put in museums
but you know they were made to be used.
The pitcher cries for water to carry
and a person for work that is real.

▪▪

From "The Summer Day," a poem by Mary Oliver:

"Tell me, what is it you plan to do with your one wild and precious life?"

▪▪

From a message by Rev. Dr. Jacqui Lewis, as quoted by the Center for Action and Contemplation (CAC):

"The core feature of a moral life is to see. Choosing not to see is immoral. The goal of religion is to improve our willingness and our ability to see. A spiritual life is supposed to help us see better. The aim of Love, and any God worth worshipping, is improved sight...

"An ethical and moral life is about letting go of indifference and *learning how to see.* It's about waking up to love ourselves, love our posse, and love our world...

"In order to live a moral life, a good life, we must commit to a life of love that means *seeing all the things.* See your neighbor suffering and do something about it. See a stranger laboring under a heavy load and help out. See lies spoken and shared in social media and call foul. See a friend soaring, and say, 'I see you, beautiful creature!' to build their self-love tank.

"Friend, you are the only one standing where you stand, seeing what you see, with your vantage point, your story. You are right there for a reason: to have, hindsight, insight, and foresight. I want us to learn to see, with our eyes wide open, how best to be healers and transformers. I want us to really see, *to fully awaken,* to the hot-mess times we are in *and* to the *incredible* power we have to love ourselves into wellness."

Heal the World
Cook Dinner Tonight

- *Penzey Spice slogan*

Margaret Wheatley discussed quantum physics in Leadership and the New Science, noting how things change and act not in isolation, but in relationship to other things. She stated that if you know *one*, and *one*, you may think you know *two,* because one and one is two. But you don't understand what the *"and"* does to it.

Wheatley said, "I believe the evolving emphasis in our society to 'think globally, act locally,' expresses a quantum perception of reality. Acting locally is a sound strategy for changing large systems. Instead of trying to map an elaborate system, the advice is to work with the system that you know, one you can get your arms around. If we look at this strategy with Newtonian eyes, we would say that we are creating incremental change. Little by little, system by system, we develop enough momentum to change the larger society. There is value in working with the system any place it manifests because unseen connections will create effects at a distance, in places we never thought."

From Rumi:

"You are not a drop in the ocean. You are the entire ocean in a drop."

Ralph Waldo Emerson, answering the question: What is success?

"To laugh often and much; to win the respect of intelligent people and the affection of children; to earn the appreciation of honest critics and endure the betrayal of false friends; to appreciate the beauty; to find the best in others; to leave the world a bit better, whether by a healthy child, a garden patch or a redeemed social condition; to know even one life has breathed easier because you have lived. This is to have succeeded!"

French author Colette wrote:

"You will do foolish things, but do them with enthusiasm."

From Mahatma Gandhi:

"When you pursue your greatest passion, you'll be amazed who you find by your side."

"Be the change you wish to see in the world."

A favorite from playwright George Bernard Shaw:

"This is the true joy in life: The being used for a purpose recognized by yourself as a mighty one. The being a force of nature, instead of a feverish, selfish little clod of ailments and grievances complaining that the world will not devote itself to making you happy. I am of the opinion that my life belongs to the whole community, and as long as I live, it is my privilege to do for it whatever I can.

"I want to be thoroughly used up when I die – for the harder I work, the more I live. I rejoice in life for its own sake. Life is no 'brief candle' to me; it is a sort of splendid torch which I have got hold of for the moment, and I want to make it burn as brightly as possible before handing it on to future generations."

And from Jim Harbaugh, University of Michigan Head Football Coach:

"Embrace each day with an enthusiasm unknown to mankind!!"

From Rumi (Mathnawi III, 1445-1449):

The Quest

Even though you're not equipped,
keep searching:
Equipment isn't necessary on the way to the Sustainer.
Whoever you see engaged in search,
become her friend and cast your head in front of her,
for choosing to be a neighbor of seekers,
you become one yourself;
Protected by conquerors,
you, yourself, learn to conquer.
If an ant seeks the rank of Solomon,
don't smile contemptuously upon its quest.
Everything you possess of skill, and wealth, and handicraft,
wasn't it first merely a thought and a quest?

From *Winnie the Pooh*, *by A. A. Milne*:

"You're braver than you believe, and stronger than you seem, and smarter than you think."

Robert Greenleaf, founder Center for Servant Leadership, defining the term:

"Who is a servant leader? One who is a servant first. It begins with the natural feeling that one wants to serve, to serve first. Then conscious choice brings one to aspire to lead. The best test is: do those served grow as persons; do they, while being served, become healthier, wiser, freer, more autonomous, more likely themselves to become servants? And, what is the effect on the least privileged in society; will they benefit?"

The Prayer of St. Francis

Lord, make me an instrument of your peace:
where there is hatred, let me sow love;
where there is injury, pardon;
where there is doubt, faith;
where there is darkness, light;
where there is sadness, joy.

O Divine Master, grant that I may
not so much seek
to be consoled as to console,
to be understood as to understand,
to be loved as to love.
For it is in giving that we receive,
it is in pardoning that we are pardoned,
and it is in dying that we are born to eternal life.

Chapter 3

Shall I Still Call Myself a Christian?

Many people now say, "I'm spiritual, but I'm not religious."

An article in *The Atlantic* (by Caroline Kitchener, January 11, 2018) stated that 65 million Americans, or 1 in 5, have rejected organized religion, but still maintain some kind of faith. Young people, especially, are rejecting the faith their parents gave them and leaving the church in droves.

I grew up in a small Iowa town, born to parents of northern European ancestry. So it is natural that I was raised a Christian, going to Sunday School, participating in Christmas and Easter pageants, going to church camp in the summers, and saying "Now I lay me down to sleep; I pray the Lord my soul to keep," at bedtime.

Being Christian was not just the church you went to; it was a fact of life, a shared set of values, a social group, a set of practices, a shared set of words. It was just there, as a backdrop of life.

In his book <u>Do I Stay Christian: A Guide for the Doubters, the Disappointed and the Disillusioned</u>, Pastor Brian McLaren wrote that this is like a child growing up in a loving, close-knit, fiercely protective family. He is told, "There is no family like our family." But then as he grows up, he starts noticing things, looks around and realizes that his family is actually part of something called the Mafia.

Some people today are almost embarrassed to say they are Christian because of the negative images we've seen of supposed "Christians" who have been judgmental, mean, unloving, and exclusionary. Religion has never had such a bad name.

What does it mean today to be a Christian? If I say I'm a Christian, does that mean I'm aligned with the people who seem to use it as a weapon for their political viewpoints? Am I complicit in the abuses committed by various church leaders? Do I have to believe everything the ministers and priests say?

These days I find myself asking Alexa to play "instrumental church hymns" so I can be soothed by the old melodies without having to quibble with the words.

So, shall I still call myself a Christian?

Pastor McLaren laid out several reasons for leaving Christianity and several for staying Christian. In the "No" column, he makes some valid points, including:

- ***Christianity's high death toll around the world***, spreading the "Doctrine of White Christian Supremacy." This ranges from the Crusades, to white Christian colonialism, to *real* witch hunts, to our own history of trying to re-culture Native Americans.
- ***Because Christianity's real master is money***. A donation-dependent religious organization is just as beholden to major donors as politicians. Why haven't white preachers spoken out more about lynchings or voter suppression? McLaren wrote, "In my mind's eye, I see Jesus flipping the tables of the money changers in the Temple. As the coins scatter across the stones, he leaves the Temple, never to return. I wonder if I should follow him out the door."

- ***Much of Christianity seems to be a white old-boys network.*** Most interpretations of the Word were made by (mostly white, European, often celibate) men. Women have been excluded from positions of power, and men have run the show. Their world hasn't exactly been safe for women, children, minorities, racial and religious minorities, or even the earth itself.
- ***Christian theology seems to be stuck***; beliefs are treated as facts and nothing is evolving. A great wall of bias has been built up in our brains. People prefer a simple lie to complex truths. We reject information that makes us uncomfortable. We believe people who seem confident – even though they may be wrong. We like stories that exonerate us, make us the heroes, and make "others" the enemy.
- ***Christianity seems to be a fading religion***. The demographics are moving it to be a faith of older people. States that have the highest participation in the Christian faith also, coincidently, have the lowest longevity rates and lowest education, income, and happiness levels.

So, if you weren't already a Christian, McLaren asks, would you be drawn to join that?? (Or, as the comedian George Carlin says, "I would never want to be a member of a group whose symbol is a man nailed to two pieces of wood.")

McLaren then makes several arguments for saying "Yes" to Christianity, including:

- ***Leaving defiantly or staying compliantly are not my only options***. I can <u>stay defiantly</u> and work for change from within. Effective change of systems comes from within. You need to know and respect the rules of any tradition and know why they exist before you can break them properly for the sake of a larger value. I don't have to go along with the old ways. I can intentionally seek out new practices that promote kindness, humility, and justice.

- ***Where else would I go?*** There is no one best church that gets it all right. Every group has real problems.
- ***The failings of the church are human failings, not failings of Christ.*** I'm human, and so are they, so "let he who is without sin cast the first stone."
- And finally, the best reason – ***because of its legendary founder, Jesus***. What he said, what he taught, what he did, how he lived. Who can argue with that?

In his book, The Road Less Traveled, M. Scott Peck wrote:

"There is clearly a lot of dirty bath water surrounding the reality of God. Holy wars. Inquisitions. Animal sacrifice. Human sacrifice. Superstition. Stultification. Dogmatism. Ignorance. Hypocrisy. Self-righteousness. Rigidity. Cruelty. Book-burning. Witch-burning. Inhibition. Fear. Conformity. Morbid guilt. Insanity. The list is almost endless. But is all this what God has done to humans or what humans have done to God?"

"I Am a Christian" by Maya Angelou

When I say … "I am a Christian"
I'm not shouting "I'm clean livin'."
I'm whispering "I was lost,
Now I'm found and forgiven."

When I say … "I am a Christian"
I don't speak of this with pride.
I'm confessing that I stumble
and need Christ to be my guide.

When I say … "I am a Christian"
I'm not trying to be strong.
I'm professing that I'm weak
And need His strength to carry on.

When I say … "I am a Christian"
I'm not bragging of success.
I'm admitting I have failed
And need God to clean my mess.

When I say … "I am a Christian"
I'm not claiming to be perfect,
My flaws are far too visible
But, God believes I am worth it.

When I say … "I am a Christian"
I still feel the sting of pain.
I have my share of heartaches
So I call upon His name.

When I say … "I am a Christian"
I'm not holier than thou,
I'm just a simple sinner
Who received God's good grace, somehow.

The late Huston Smith was a leading scholar of religious studies and wrote several books on the world's religions and philosophies. When studying a religion, he immersed himself in the culture and life of that religion so as to better understand it. Smith was the subject of a great Bill Moyers series called *The Wisdom of Faith*. In his book The World's Religions, Smith wrote about the core messages of Christianity:

> Jesus invited us to see differently. We are told that we are not to resist evil but to turn the other cheek. The world assumes that evil must be resisted by every means available.
>
> We are told to love our enemies and bless those who curse us. The world assumes that friends are to be loved and enemies hated.
>
> We are told that the sun rises on the just and the unjust alike. The world considers this undiscriminating; it would like to see clouds over evil people and is offended when they go unpunished.
>
> We are told that outcasts and harlots enter the kingdom of God before many who are perfunctorily righteous. Again unfair, the world thinks; respectable people should head the procession.
>
> We are told that the happy people are those who are meek, who weep, who are merciful and pure in heart. The world assumes that it is the rich, the powerful, and the wellborn who are happy.
>
> Everything that came from his lips formed the surface of a burning glass to focus human awareness on the two most important facts about life: God's overwhelming love of humanity, and the need for people to accept that love and let it flow through them to others.

> The most impressive thing about the teachings of Jesus is not that he taught them but that he appears to have lived them.

So, have we gotten the core message of Christianity all wrong??

When telling future leaders to pay attention to the four dimensions of their life (Physical, Intellectual, Social/ Emotional, and Spiritual), my partner, Tim Quinn, has always given this advice:

"Never let any man's religion get between you and your own spirit."

Martin Luther King, Jr., was quoted as saying:

"11 a.m. on Sunday morning is the most segregated hour in Christian America."

Richard Rohr, a Franciscan priest, wrote a very thought-provoking book, The Universal Christ: How a Forgotten Reality Can Change Everything We See, Hope For, and Believe*. It is worth reading in its entirety, but here are a few key ideas that struck me.*

In the book, he reminds us that *Christ* is not Jesus' last name, but the title for his life's purpose. Christ is our word for what Jesus came to personally reveal and validate. Christ is the spiritual energy in the world. All things are the revelation of God's endlessly diffusive spiritual energy.

Rohr states that Jesus is a Third Someone, not just God and not just man, but God and human together. But humans have turned this original idea into a competitive theology. Millions are waiting for the "Second Coming" having largely missed the first and its meaning and messages.

"Christ is a good and simple metaphor for absolute wholeness, complete incarnation, and the integrity of creation. Jesus is the archetypal human just like us who showed us what the Full Human might look like if we could fully live into it. Frankly, Jesus came to show us how to be human much more than how to be spiritual."

Rohr says Christianity's core good news is that *you are able to share the divine nature*. This implies:

- God is not an old man on a throne. God is Relationship itself, a dynamism of Infinite Love, as the doctrine of the Trinity demonstrates.
- God's infinite love has always included all that God created from the very beginning.
- That the Divine DNA of the Creator is therefore held in all the creatures. What we call the soul of every creature could easily be seen as the self-knowledge of God in that creature.

Rohr states, "You have to trust the messenger before you can trust the message, and that seems to be the Jesus Christ strategy. Too often, we have substituted the messenger for the message. Too often this obsession became a pious substitute for actually following what he taught – and he did ask us several times to follow him, and never once to worship him. He says Christianity should be a lifestyle – a way of being in the world that is simple, non-violent, shared, and loving. However, we've made it into an established religion and avoided the lifestyle change itself. One can be greedy, warlike, racist, selfish, and vain, yet still believe that Jesus is one's personal Lord and Savior."

In the Apostles' Creed, Rohr says there is "The Great Comma." The Creed says, "I believe in Jesus Christ…who was conceived by the Holy Spirit, born of the Virgin Mary, suffered under Pontius Pilate, was crucified, died…." Rohr stated, "The Creed makes a huge leap between his birth and death, and everything Jesus said and did is ignored. It does not once mention love, service, hope, the least of the brothers and sisters, or even forgiveness – anything, actually that is remotely actionable. It's a vision and philosophy statement, with no mission statement attached."

On the Crucifixion and the Resurrection:

For most of Christian history, there has not been much agreement on what it means to say, "Jesus died for our sins." *(Note: I even remember arguing with our pastor about this in communion class when I was 13 because the concept just didn't make sense to me.)* Rohr says that this is often referred to as the "penal substitutionary atonement theory." It theorizes that Christ, by his own sacrificial choice, was punished in the place of us sinners. But, he says, this is just a theory, just like "original sin." This whole theory has dominated the Christian narrative, often much more than his life and teaching. This causes us to largely "thank" Jesus instead of honestly imitating him.

He says, "The crucifixion of Jesus – whom we see as the Son of God – was a devastating prophecy that humans would sooner kill God than change themselves.

"We need to enlarge our view of resurrection – from a one-time miracle in the life of Jesus that asks for assent and belief – to a pattern of creation that has always been true, and that invites us to much more than belief in a miracle. Resurrection is another word for change, but particularly positive change – which we tend to see only in the long run. In the short run, it often just looks like death."

Rohr eloquently states, "The cross is the standing statement of what we do to one another and to ourselves. The resurrection is the standing statement of what God does to us in return... Christ Crucified is all of the hidden, private, tragic pain of history made public and given over to God. Christ Resurrected is all suffering received, loved, and transformed by an all-caring God. How else could we have any kind of cosmic hope? How else would we not die of sadness for what humanity has done to itself and what we have done to one another?"

Maybe Christians are not as much leaving Christianity as they are realigning with groups that live Christian values in the world. It is not the brand name that matters.

Rohr thinks that if we can remember that we all came from God and are headed back to God, whatever circuitous route we take, it will help us be more humble and patient with each other. "We all have our preferred symbols, rituals, Scriptures, and words for things, but let's not ever let them get in the way of what they are all pointing to and leading us toward – union of the soul with God."

"A mature Christian sees Christ in everything and everyone else. That is a definition that will never fail you, always demand more of you, and give you no reasons to fight, exclude, or reject anyone."

Chapter 4

What are Lessons from Other Religions?

According to Wikipedia, approximately one-third of the world's almost 8 billion people are of the Christian faith. Does that mean that the other 5 billion are just plain wrong about everything? Are they all "heathens" who are going to "go to hell" when they die?

Or, am I missing an opportunity to learn something important from other religions and other perspectives? What are some of the key tenets of other faiths that seem true to me?

Are some religious practices and rituals "better than" others? Or, are the world's organized religions just different window dressings for the same spiritual truth?

What follows is not a complete survey, summary, or evaluation of other religions. Rather, it is some thoughts from or about other religions I've come across that have given me something to ponder.

In his book, <u>The World's Religions</u>, Huston Smith made this point:

"It is possible to climb life's mountain from any side, but when the top is reached, all trails converge. At base, in the foothills of theology, ritual, and organizational structure, the religions are distinct. Differences in culture, history, geography, and collective temperament all make for diverse starting points. Far from being deplorable, this is good. The various major religions are alternate paths to the same goal.

Those who circle the mountain, trying to bring others around to their paths, are not climbing. People in ignorance say, 'My religion is the only one, my religion is the best.' But when a heart is illumined by true knowledge, it knows that above all these wars of sects and sectarians presides the one indivisible, eternal, all-knowing bliss."

■■

In the book of meditations, Yes, And..., Fr. Richard Rohr says:

"I can't believe that God expects all humans to start from zero and reinvent the wheel of life in their own small lifetimes. We must build on the common and inherited wisdom of the ages. This broadens the field from 'my religion, which has the whole truth,' to 'universal wisdom, which my religion teaches in this way.' If it is true, then it has to be true everywhere. Many themes keep recurring in different religions and with different metaphors. But the foundational wisdom is usually the same."

■■

After studying the world's religions in depth, Huston Smith stated that, "If we take the world's enduring religions at their very best, we have the distilled wisdom of the human race." In The World's Religions, he said that if you pass a strainer through the world's religions and lift out their conclusions about reality and how life should be lived (leaving the extraneous stuff out), you begin to see what looks like the winnowed wisdom of the human race:

First, Ethics. Avoid murder, thieving, lying and adultery. Minimum guidelines, but they are not nothing, as we reflect on how much better the world would be if they were universally honored.

Second, Virtues. Move on into the kind of people we should become. Three basic virtues are found universally – humility, charity, and veracity. ***Humility*** is the capacity to regard oneself in the company of others as one, but not more than one. ***Charity*** shifts that shoe to the other foot; it is to regard one's neighbor as likewise one, as fully one as oneself. ***Veracity*** extends beyond truth-telling to objectivity – the capacity to see things as they really are, to live authentically.

Third, Vision, which is the wisdom traditions' rendering of the ultimate character of things. The unified wholeness of everything; that reality is more integrated than it seems, better than it seems, and more mysterious than you could ever imagine. This is the highest common denominator of the wisdom traditions. When we add to this the baseline they establish for ethical behavior and their account of the human virtues, a pretty wise platform for life has been described.

At the center of religious life is a particular kind of joy, the prospect of a happy ending that blossoms from necessarily painful beginnings, the promise of human difficulties embraced and overcome.

Huston Smith also discusses the commonalities of the world's various religious practices. (The World's Religions) He says six aspects of organized religion surface so regularly as to suggest that their seeds are in the human makeup.

1. ***Authority***. Leaving divine authority aside and seeking the advice of people who are above average in these matters. Religion's institutional, organized side calls for administrative bodies and individuals who occupy positions of authority, whose decisions carry weight.

2. ***Ritual.*** When we're crushed by loss, or exuberant with joy, we want to be with people and interact with them in ways that tie us together.
3. ***Explanations***. Religion may begin as ritual, but we soon want explanations about where we come from, where we go.
4. ***Tradition***. In humans, it is tradition more than instinct that conserves what past generations have learned and pass on to the present generation.
5. ***Grace.*** The belief – often hard to sustain in the face of facts – that Reality is ultimately on our side, that the universe is friendly, that we can feel at home in it. Religion says that the best things are the more eternal things.
6. ***Mystery***. Religion traffics in mystery. The human mind cannot begin to fathom the Infinite it is drawn to.

Smith says that religion will always be ambiguous. We don't really want life to give us all the answers, because that takes away our freedom. Religion can provide maps and guidelines, but not all the answers.

Scientific methods can tell us some aspects of reality, he says, but they can't tell us all. We can't test religion in the lab – we can't even comprehend the variables we'd have to test for. He provides the analogy of dogs not being able to comprehend all of our capabilities; they would need to subject everything to a "sniff" test.

Oprah Winfrey's book, The Wisdom of Sundays, is a compilation of the best ideas from conversations with her many guests on the OWN series "Super Soul Sunday." Here are a couple thoughts on the difference between spirituality and religion:

Elizabeth Lesser said, "Spirituality is this kind of fearless seeking nature. It's the part of us that says, Whoa. What made a tree? Who am I? Where did I come from? What made something out of nothing? Where do I go when I die? How do I live? How am I supposed to live? That's spirituality. The seeking of truth. Religions are our attempt to answer the questions. And some of those answers are great and beautiful. And some of them are just dogma and rules that get us into trouble. 'My rules are better than your rules.' And then we fight about them. So spirituality is the questioning, and religions are our attempts at answers."

Iyanla Vanzant stated, "Religion is the rules, regulation, ceremonies, and rituals developed by man to create conformity and uniformity in the approach to God. Spirituality is God's call in your soul."

***Untitled**, by Philip Appleman*

O Karma, Dharma, pudding and pie,
Gimme a break before I die:
grant me wisdom, will & wit,
purity, probity, pluck, & grit.
Trustworthy, loyal, helpful, kind,
gimme great abs & a steel-trap mind,
and forgive, Ye Gods, some humble advice—
these little blessings would suffice
to beget an earthly paradise:
make the bad people good—
and the good people nice;
and before our world goes over the brink,
teach the believers how to think.

Thoughts from Hinduism

One of the world's oldest religions, and one far from my realm of experience, is Hinduism. It is the world's third-largest religion, with over 1.2 billion followers, most of whom live in India. In The World's Religions, Huston Smith stated that if compressed into a single affirmation, we would find Hinduism saying: You can have what you want. But what does man want? People want four things:

1. ***Pleasure***. They begin by wanting pleasure – beauty, delight. As long as the basic rules of morality are obeyed, you are free to seek all the pleasure you want. Seek it intelligently.
2. But then pleasure is not enough and is too trivial to satisfy one's total nature. So the next thing the individual turns to, the second major goal in life, is ***worldly success*** – wealth, fame and power. Again, a worthy goal. A measure of success is needed to support a household and discharge civic duties responsibly and have self-respect. But if this is your chief ambition, you'll never be satisfied. Wealth, fame, and power don't survive bodily death – you can't take it with you.
3. When that becomes not enough, the will to ***get*** turns into the will to ***serve.*** You seek duty and service to others.
4. But pleasure, success, and duty are never humanity's ultimate goals. They are a means to getting us to what we really want: ***Infinite Being*** (no one wants to die), ***Infinite Knowledge*** (what it all means), and ***Infinite Joy***. This is the infinite center of every life, this hidden self or Atman, which is no less than Brahman, the godhead. It is seeking to unite your human spirit with the God who lies within.

(Note: To me, this makes some sense and sounds vaguely like a "Maslow's Hierarchy of Needs" for the spirit. Abraham Maslow's widely-used Theory of Human Motivation describes the five stages of human needs: Physiological, Safety, Love and Belongness, Self Esteem, and Self-Actualization. He later added Transcendence.)

Hinduism is a many-layered religion that I can only scratch the surface of. Ideas such as karma, dharma, the caste system, and reincarnation have come from Hinduism, but have often been misinterpreted by Westerners.

Mahatma Gandhi, non-violent civil rights leader from India, wrote:

"God has no religion. I believe in the fundamental truth of all great religions of the world."

Thoughts from Buddhism

Buddha (Siddhartha Gautama) was born around 563 BC in what is now Nepal, in the Himalayan mountains. Buddha means the Awakened One, or the enlightened One. His father was a king, or feudal lord, so he grew up with all kinds of riches. But he became discontented in his 20's and abandoned everything to spend six years in the forest, searching for the answers to life's big questions. He found Enlightenment, then spent almost 50 years traveling, teaching, training monks, and comforting. Buddha is viewed as a teacher, not a god.

Huston Smith said that the religion of Buddhism grew out of Hinduism, kind of like a Protestant movement. In it are Four Noble Truths:

1. To be human is to experience suffering – birth, sickness, decrepitude, fear of death, separation from what one loves, being tied to what one dislikes.
2. The cause of suffering is desire and attachment.
3. If the cause of suffering is craving, we can be relieved of suffering by overcoming such craving.
4. The way to do this is through the Eightfold Path.

The Noble Eightfold Path, that leads to the extinction of suffering is this:

1. Right Understanding
2. Right Thought
3. Right Speech (abstaining from lying, harsh language, vain talk)
4. Right Action (no killing, lying, stealing, etc.)
5. Right Livelihood (making your living in an honest way)
6. Right Effort
7. Right Mindfulness
8. Right Concentration

Buddhism teaches that grace comes by intense self-work now, rather than by redemption later. There are multiple ways to God, and some ways may work better for some people. A yoga is a practice that can help the individual on that path. According to Buddhism, the world's purpose is to provide a kind of training ground for the human spirit.

"Dalai Lama" is the title given by Tibetan people to the foremost spiritual leader of Tibetan Buddhism. The Dalai Lama XIV stated:

"My religion is very simple. My religion is kindness."

I've often heard the Hebrew word "shalom." But I never really thought about what it meant. So, I went to that definitive source, Google, to find out. Google gave me a great answer:

"*Shalom* is a greeting used by Jewish people when greeting or parting that translates to 'peace.'

"But there are layers of meaning to the word 'shalom' beyond a simple greeting, or peace as the absence of war. Peace is a wholeness with God, a completeness, well-being, where nothing is lacking in you. It is something like shorthand for saying, 'May you be filled with a complete and perfect peace and be full of well-being,' or 'May health, prosperity, and peace of mind and spirit be upon you.' Beyond being just a simple wish for peace and happiness, the word suggests a state of fullness and perfection, overflowing inner and outer joy, and peaceful serenity.

"The word *shalom* or *peace* is used 200 times in the Bible, so it must have meant something. Simply hearing the greeting 'shalom' can be a reminder of the deep human longing for peace, for a true peace that is greater than all understanding."

Thoughts from Islam

In his chapter on Islam in <u>The World's Religions</u>, Huston Smith said that Islam has been bastardized, misused, or misunderstood as much as Christianity. The religion was built on Judaism and Christianity as a base. But its premise is that Christ's work was unfinished, so it tells us how to live and apply

Christianity's principles. Smith's description of Islam includes the following:

Islam says there is no god but Allah (the Arabic word for God), and Muhammad is God's messenger. (Muhammad lived in Saudi Arabia from 570 – 632 CE.) It is believed that the Koran was sent directly from God to Muhammad; it was written in Arabic, so multiple language translations over time have not occurred, like in Christianity. The Koran is a book emphasizing deeds, rather than ideas. It embodies the beautiful sentiments of Jesus in definite laws, which did serve to greatly improve civilization at the time in the Middle East. It includes many social teachings. Some of the more objectionable interpretations (to our eyes) are local customs rather than strict Koranic law. This is because people are people, and like any other religion, it has been misapplied or misinterpreted for personal gain.

Islam says people have two obligations – first, gratitude for the life that has been received. The second is surrender to Allah (the only God) so you're not a slave to everything else. The five daily prayers are to keep lives in focus – to give thanks and keep your life in perspective.

The observance of the holy month of Ramadan requires fasting from sunup to sundown. Its purpose is to make one think, teach self-discipline, underscore our dependence on God, and sensitize compassion.

We in the West think of the phrase "Allahu Akbar" as a battle cry for Muslim extremists and terrorists. But its true meaning is that *God is greatest*, or *God is greater*. It is the beginning of the daily Muslim prayers.

▪▪

Rumi was a great mystic poet of Islam. He was born in 1207 is what is now Afghanistan and died in southern Turkey in 1273, leaving behind prolific writings that explored all the nuances of human character, good/evil, and the drama of the soul's journey to God. (from Andrew Harvey, The Rumi Collection). Rumi wrote:

> I searched for God among the Christians and on the Cross and therein I found Him not.
> I went into the ancient temples of idolatry; no trace of Him was there.
> I entered the mountain cave of Hira and then went as far as Qandhar but God I found not.
> Then I directed my search to the Kaaba, the resort of old and young; God was not there even.
> Turning to philosophy I inquired about him from Ibn Sina but found Him not.
> I fared then to the scene of the Prophet's experience of a great divine manifestation only a "two bow-lengths' distance from him" but God was not there even in that exalted court.
> Finally, I looked into my own heart and there I saw Him; He was nowhere else.

Mystical thoughts from Deepak Chopra (Why is God Laughing?):

“Each of us is here to discover our true selves; that essentially we are spiritual beings who have taken manifestation in physical form; that we're not human beings who have occasional spiritual experiences, but we're spiritual beings that have occasional human experiences.

“Either you're a person wondering if you have a soul, or you're a soul who knows that being a person isn't real.”

Unitarian congregations are attracting people from various beliefs and backgrounds. From the Unitarian Universalist Association web site, www.uua.org:

Unitarian Universalist congregations affirm and promote seven Principles, which are held as strong values and moral guides. Unitarians aspire to live out these Principles within a "living tradition" of wisdom and spirituality, drawn from sources as diverse as science, poetry, scripture, and personal experience. The Principles are not dogma or doctrine, but rather a guide for people who choose to join and participate in Unitarian Universalist religious communities.

1st Principle: The inherent worth and dignity of every person;
2nd Principle: Justice, equity and compassion in human relations;
3rd Principle: Acceptance of one another and encouragement to spiritual growth in our congregations;
4th Principle: A free and responsible search for truth and meaning;
5th Principle: The right of conscience and the use of the democratic process within our congregations and in society at large;
6th Principle: The goal of world community with peace, liberty, and justice for all;
7th Principle: Respect for the interdependent web of all existence of which we are a part.

There are six sources UUA congregations affirm and promote:

- Direct experience of that transcending mystery and wonder, affirmed in all cultures, which moves us to a renewal of the spirit and an openness to the forces which create and uphold life;

- Words and deeds of prophetic people which challenge us to confront powers and structures of evil with justice, compassion, and the transforming power of love;
- Wisdom from the world's religions which inspires us in our ethical and spiritual life;
- Jewish and Christian teachings which call us to respond to God's love by loving our neighbors as ourselves;
- Humanist teachings which counsel us to heed the guidance of reason and the results of science, and warn us against idolatries of the mind and spirit;
- Spiritual teachings of Earth-centered traditions which celebrate the sacred circle of life and instruct us to live in harmony with the rhythms of nature.

Lyrics from "Imagine," by John Lennon:

Imagine there's no heaven
It's easy if you try
No hell below us
Above us only sky
Imagine all the people
Living for today

Imagine there's no countries
It isn't hard to do
Nothing to kill or die for
And no religion too
Imagine all the people
Living life in peace

You may say I'm a dreamer
But I'm not the only one

I hope someday you'll join us
And the world will be as one

Final Thoughts on Other Religions

From Mark Twain:

"The easy confidence with which I know another man's religion is folly teaches me to suspect that my own is also."

From Huston Smith:

"The Perennial Tradition, which most world religions have stated in different ways, somehow says that a person's final end is union with God and all things. This is the simple goal of our existence. If your religion is not helping you to do that, then you better get a new religion."

From Marianne Williamson:

"Just like a sunbeam can't separate itself from the sun, and a wave can't separate itself from the ocean, we can't separate ourselves from one another. We are all part of a vast sea of love, one indivisible divine mind."

From Richard Rohr ("Finding it in Nature," January 19, 2015):

"Question #3 of The New Baltimore Catechism was 'Why did God make me?' And the answer was simple, true, and enough for a lifetime of meaning: 'God made us to show forth his goodness and to share with us his everlasting happiness in heaven.'

"Really think about that and what it means for your life."

From Eckhart Tolle, in Guardians of Being:

"The animals give God glory just through their simple existence. Ducks do the duck thing, squirrels do the squirrel thing without any resistance to themselves or envy of the other. We have forgotten what rocks, plants, and animals still know. We have forgotten how to be – to be still, to be ourselves, to be where life is: Here and Now. . . . What is it that so many people find enchanting in animals? Their essence – their Being – is not covered up by the mind, as it is in most humans."

From author Anne Lamott:

"We must know that creation is our first and final cathedral. Nature is the one song of praise that never stops singing, as many of the Psalms say. If you are drawn to 'kneel' in this cathedral, you can always talk to a Mystery that is so much larger than yourself. It takes no theology classes whatsoever, no proofs, or arguments. Aweism is the one true religion. All the other native and historical religions merely build upon this primal awe that bows before everything."

Chapter 5

Why am I Drawn to Celtic Christian Spirituality?

I have always felt closest to my spirit when taking a walk in the woods or on the beach. The natural sounds, sights, and smells of nature always soothe my soul. How can you stay all wrapped up in your own ego when you look at the trees in the forest or all the stars in the night sky? You know there is something bigger going on that is absolutely incredible, and you feel connected to it.

At the same time, maybe partly because of my Scottish ancestry, I've been drawn to ancient stone circles, Celtic writings and poetry. There is mystery there, and ancient wisdom.

Who were the early Celts? Living in Scotland, Ireland and Wales, how did they come to adopt the Christian faith? What are the beliefs and practices? Unlike the Lutheran, Methodist, Catholic, and other church denominations, there is no official organization or hierarchy of Celtic Christian churches to codify everything. It seems to be sort of an "underground" or grass roots spiritual practice.

When we think of religion in Ireland, we usually think of "The Troubles" and the deep divisions between the Catholics and the Protestants. Journalist Frank McNally wrote, "Ireland remains a deeply religious country, with the two main denominations being 'us' and 'them.'" *(Irish Times 3/11/98)* But there is a third option to consider and learn from – Celtic Christian spirituality.

Here are some thoughts I've gathered about Celtic spirituality that have made sense to me.

The Celtic Center shares the following about Celtic spirituality (thecelticcenter.org):

"Because the Celtic people were a bit out of the reach of the Roman Empire and the Roman Church, they were far less influenced by those political and religious systems. This isolation allowed them to maintain their ancient and time-honored practices regarding the dignity of nature and community, the equality of men and women, and their vibrant and poetic imaginations as portals to understanding human beings as well as God. As Christianity arrived to these cultures and communities, they were able, for many centuries, to find a beautiful synthesis of these ancient practices and beliefs with the Christian understanding of God's message of Divine presence and eternal belonging for everyone.

"Although no culture contains truth completely or perfectly, the early Christian Celts were able to see the beautiful presence of the Divine in a relationship with Nature that stressed humility, dignity of all things, and God's presence in and through all of Creation. They maintained rich spiritual practices such as prayer, meditation, communing with Nature, care for those in need, hospitality, and poetic use of the imagination and art. They saw, in all experiences, the presence of the Spirit, and were very skilled at seeking encounter with God in all of life. The Celts believed men and women are equally able to inspire, lead, and participate in all aspects of community and spiritual practice. And they had a wonderful tradition of cultivating soul-friends who took caring responsibility for assisting in the development of and sustained journey of a spiritual life well lived."

▪▪

"A Simple Guide to Celtic Spirituality and Nature," (vbchange.com/celtic-spirituality) says:

"The link between nature and Celtic spirituality is great. The Celts have a firm belief in the following statement, 'If you wish to understand the creator, first understand his creation.'

"In this way, as the Celts search for the answers they are looking for towards spiritual completion, they do so through appreciating and understanding nature."

▪▪

From Richard Rohr's September 31, 2020 daily meditation (Center for Action and Contemplation):

"On the margins of the Roman Empire, Ireland and Scotland helped hand down the Christian contemplative lineage. The Romans had conquered much of Europe by the time of Jesus' birth; though they ruled Britain, the Romans never occupied Ireland or parts of Scotland. This allowed the Celtic culture and Christian monks the freedom to thrive independently. They weren't controlled by Roman practicality or Greek thinking. When Christian missionaries arrived by the third century, the Celts blended their pagan or creation-based spirituality with Christian liturgy, practice, and structure. As a result, Celtic Christianity was still grounded in the natural world, and they had much easier access to a cosmic notion of the Christ.

"Perhaps we can think of Celtic Christians as an alternative community on the edge of the inside of organized Christianity. Lacking the structure and support of the organized church, radical forms of Christianity never thrive for very long. Without the Irish monks, much of Celtic practice and thought would not have been passed on to us at all.

"Like the Desert Fathers and Mothers who influenced them, Celtic mystics focused on rather different things than the mainstream church. The Celts drew on their own cultural symbols and experience to emphasize other values than the symbols of 'Roman' Catholicism. For example, Celtic Christianity encouraged the practice of confession to an anam cara (soul friend) more than to an ordained priest.

"They also saw God as a deep kind of listening and speaking presence, as in 'The Deer's Cry.' I invite you to read this excerpt of St. Patrick's traditional prayer slowly, and to allow yourself, like the ancient Celts, to become aware of the presence of Christ surrounding you through all things."

The Lorica of St. Patrick (The Deer`s Cry)

I arise to-day:
vast might, invocation of the Trinity,—
belief in a Threeness
confession of Oneness
meeting in the Creator. . . .

I arise to-day:
might of Heaven
brightness of Sun
whiteness of Snow
splendour of Fire
speed of Light
swiftness of Wind

depth of Sea
stability of Earth
firmness of Rock.

I arise to-day:
Might of God for my piloting
Wisdom of God for my guidance
Eye of God for my foresight
Ear of God for my hearing
Word of God for my utterance
Hand of God for my guardianship
Path of God for my precedence
Shield of God for my protection
Host of God for my salvation . . .

Christ with me, Christ before me,
Christ behind me, Christ in me,
Christ under me, Christ over me,
Christ to right of me, Christ to left of me,
Christ in lying down, Christ in sitting, Christ in rising up
Christ in the heart of every person, who may think of me!
Christ in the mouth of every one, who may speak to me!
Christ in every eye, which may look on me!
Christ in every ear, which may hear me!

I arise to-day:
vast might, invocation of the Trinity
belief in a Threeness
confession of Oneness
meeting in the Creator.

Excerpted *From 12 Celtic Spiritual Practices to Celebrate God in Our World," US Catholic, Christine Valters Painter 5/21/19:*

Celtic Christian spirituality refers to a set of practices and beliefs in Ireland, Scotland and Wales that evolved in the 5th century. Many practices have roots in desert spirituality or Celtic pre-Christian culture dating back to 500 BC. Key is the idea that the natural world reveals the sacramentality of all creation. Here are a few of the practices they suggest could be adapted:

Thresholds. Thresholds are the spaces between when we move from one time to another, as in the threshold of dawn to day or dusk to dark; from one space to another; and in times when old structures start to fall away and we begin to envision something new. The Celtic peoples had a love of edges and boundary places, most likely as the result of living on islands. In daily life, become aware each time you cross a threshold. This might be in moving from one activity to another, or at dawn and dusk. Pause at each of these and offer a short prayer of gratitude.

Dreams. In ancient times dreams were respected as signs from God. Dreams also play a significant role in scripture, with guidance and direction often arriving in these night visions. In daily life, place a journal and pen by your bed at night and then ask God for a dream before sleep. Even if you awaken with only a fragment or a feeling, record it.

Blessing each moment. In the Celtic tradition, one of the practices that aids in daily life is blessing, or prayers celebrating the ordinary tasks of the day. Blessing is an act of acknowledging the gifts and graces already present and offering gratitude to God for them. All the mundane activities of the day are opportunities to witness grace at work. In daily life, see the everyday things of our lives as openings into the depths of the world. The steam rising from my coffee, the bird singing from a tree branch outside my window, the meal that nourishes my body all bring me closer to God's grace. Consider saying a blessing of gratitude for each of the ordinary things that sustain you during the day.

Soul friendship. Another key practice for the Celtic saints was having a soul friend. Everyone, whether lay or clergy, man or woman, was expected to have a spiritual mentor and companion on the soul's journey. This was a person in whom they could confide all of their inner struggles and help in finding their path. There was a sense of genuine warmth and intimacy in this relationship and deep respect for the other's wisdom as a source of blessing. Age or gender differences did not matter. In daily life, seek out a soul friend. You may already have one in your life: a spiritual director, a wise guide, someone you can turn to when things feel challenging and to whom you entrust the secret desires of your heart.

Walking the rounds. A central Celtic practice at sacred sites, such as churches, graves, and crosses, is known as "walking the rounds." This involves walking sunwise (or clockwise) in a mindful way around various markers or monuments, often three times to reflect the sacredness of that number in the Celtic imagination. Walking helps to arrive to a place and slow down. Walking in a circular manner helps to move us out of linear ways of thinking and to open our hearts to receive God's grace.

Solitude and silence. The desert tradition profoundly influenced the Celtic monks; while many monks were unable to go to the literal desert, they sought out the wild edges and solitary places of wilderness. There are many sacred places in Ireland and Wales with the word *dysert* or *disert* in the name. This is the Gaelic word for *desert* and refers to a place of solitude and silence, a retreat for those who long for a more intimate encounter with God and where attention can be cultivated with few distractions. In daily life, begin by making a commitment to spending time each day in silence. Turn off any notifications from your phone or computer and ask others in your house not to disturb you.

Seasonal cycles. The unfolding of the seasons was an overarching template for the Celtic imagination. In the pre-Christian tradition there are significant feast days aligned with the equinoxes and solstices. The Christian calendar incorporates many of these rhythms, with Christmas falling near the winter solstice, the feast of John the Baptist at the summer solstice, and Easter after the spring equinox. In daily life, make time for contemplative walks outside. Pay attention to the world around you and to the signs of the season – what flowers might be in bloom, whether the trees have their leaves, and the height of the sun in the sky. Ask yourself what season your own soul is in right now.

Nature as revelation. The Celtic imagination considers sacred places to be "thin," or places where the veil between the worlds, meaning heaven and earth, seem especially near to each other. Ninth-century Irish theologian John Scotus Eriugena taught that there are two books of revelation: the book of the scriptures and the book of creation. Both are required to know the fullness of the divine presence. The Celtic monks sought out places in the wilderness to receive these gifts of revelation. In daily life, make a commitment to spend time in nature and be present to it as a place of revelation.

Three essential things. Three is a sacred number in the Celtic tradition, and often the saints expressed their own desires or commitments in terms of the number three. What is essential to one person will be different to another. Similarly in different seasons of life, what is essential for us might change. In daily life, reflect on the three things in your own life you count as most essential. Hold them as principles or touchstones for your life right now as you continue your spiritual journey. One way to do this is to imagine you are at the end of your life looking back. For what do you want to be remembered?

Mary Meighan, founder of Celtic Journeys, a provider of Celtic spiritual retreats in Ireland, has a talk on YouTube. In it, she offers the following:

"Celts were first pagans. When Christianity came, it took a different form than in other European countries that had been invaded by the Romans. Celts assimilated Christianity and put it on top of their beliefs. It is more an everyday spirituality, weaving the ordinary with the mystical.

"In the practice of Celtic Christianity, nothing is too ordinary to give a blessing to. That is why you'll find literally thousands of blessings, and hundreds of books of Irish blessings. (Starting your day with a blessing is an incredibly different way than starting with a to-do list.)

"The Irish saw God's handiwork in everything about them. Their livelihood, life, everything was dependent on God's will. It was only natural, then, to ask for God's blessing and help in every aspect of everyday life. That's why you'll find blessings for:

- Hearing the cock crow
- Seeing the sun
- Lighting the fire
- Going out and about
- Making bread
- Milking the cow
- A backache
- Going to sea

- Taking snuff at a wake
- The dead
- Seeing the new moon"

Who was St. Brigid? Wikipedia says:

St. Brigid, or "Mary of the Gael," may be the true patron saint of Ireland. She is more Irish than St. Patrick, who was Welsh. According to legend, she was both a pagan goddess and a Christian saint. She is the "midwife" of our souls. When undergoing transformation, she is a threshold saint/person, helping our transition. St. Brigid's flame burns continually in Kildare, Ireland, a symbol of burning off things that need to go and lighting the way for that which is coming. February 1 is celebrated as St. Brigid's Day. St. Brigid's Cross is traditionally woven from straw.

St. Brigid's Cross

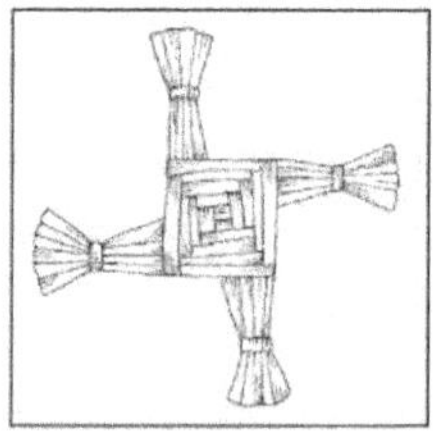

From Anam Cara: Spiritual Wisdom from the Celtic World, by John O'Donohue:

"Friendship is the sweet grace which liberates us to approach, recognize and inhabit this adventure of life. If the human journey is approached in a spirit of friendship, the unknown, the anonymous, the negative and the threatening gradually yield their secret affinity to us.

"Celtic spirituality shows the inner friendship which embraces nature, divinity, underworld and human world as one. An imaginative and unifying friendship is the Celtic gift. Your self, your body, others, death.... It was all shown to be your anam cara – a friend to your soul."

A Friendship Blessing

May you be blessed with good friends.
May you learn to be a good friend to your self.
May you be able to journey to that place in your soul where there is great love, warmth, feeling and forgiveness.
May this change you.
May it transfigure that which is negative, distant or cold in you.
May you be brought in to the real passion, kinship and affinity of belonging.
May you treasure your friends.
May you be good to them and may you be there for them; may they bring you all the blessings, challenges, truth and light that you need for your journey.
May you never be isolated; but may you always be in the gentle nest of belonging with your anam cara.

Chapter 6

Do I Have to Believe Everything I've Been Taught?

If my "path up the mountain" is through the basic lens of Christianity, how do I reconcile some of the teachings of the church that don't feel right to me? Is it OK to question or disagree?

How am I to interpret seemingly contradictory teachings of the Bible? Do I have to accept that everything the Bible says is literally true?

Is there really a Heaven and a Hell, or are these metaphors for consequences of behavior? What does it really mean to be "saved from your sins?"

Do I have to go to church to be a "good Christian?"

Thoughts On the Bible

Fr. Richard Rohr in his meditations and his book Yes, and... wrote:

"To take the Scriptures seriously is not to take them literally. Literalism is the lowest and least level of meaning. For too long we've used and cherry-picked the Bible merely to support various church positions. Bible text became handy ammunition. We selectively chose some texts while avoiding others – resulting in slavery, racism, homophobia, sexism, etc. lasting into our time.

"But Jesus went deeper and taught what should be seen, emphasized, what could be de-emphasized or even ignored. He ignored or even denied exclusionary, punitive texts in favor of passages that emphasized inclusion, mercy, and honesty. We must be honest that the New Testament was written largely in Greek – a language which Jesus did not speak or understand – thirty to seventy years after his death. We can only conclude that the exact words of Jesus were apparently not that important for the Holy Spirit – or for us.

"It takes a certain level of human and spiritual maturity to interpret a Scripture. Vengeful and petty people find vengeful and petty texts. Loving and peaceful people will hold out until a text resounds deep within them.

"The Bible is not an answer book, so we can somehow 'know' God as an intellectual exercise. It is only in walking the journey of faith, hope, and love itself that we come to know the real answers. It is vital to realize that no single passage of the Bible can be taken in isolation from the others. The fact is, if we simply go searching after 'proof texts,' we can assert anything we want from the Scriptures.

"The Bible was written in faith and it can be understood only in faith. In other words, it cannot be read cynically (liberals) nor literally (conservatives), which are merely two different forms of rationalism to keep ourselves in control. Our faith is not in the *words* of the Bible. Our faith is in the Triune God who is very subtly and slowly revealing the Divine Mystery in space and time – and yes through words and stories, parables and biographies."

▪▪▪

Richard Dawkins, author of The God Delusion, wrote:

"To be fair, much of the Bible is not systematically evil but just plain weird, as you would expect of a chaotically cobbled-together anthology of disjointed documents, composed, revised, translated, distorted and 'improved' by hundreds of anonymous authors, editors and copyists, unknown to us and mostly unknown to each other, spanning nine centuries."

From To Kill a Mockingbird, Harper Lee:

"Sometimes the Bible in the hand of one man is worse than a whisky bottle in the hand of (another)... There are just some kind of men who - who're so busy worrying about the next world they've never learned to live in this one, and you can look down the street and see the results."

Thoughts On Prayer

Tilden Edwards, a spiritual teacher and co-founder of The Shalem Institute, described the purpose of prayer:

"Authentic prayer is opening to God's gracious presence with all that we are, with what Scripture summarizes as our whole heart, soul, and mind (Matthew 22:37). Therefore, prayer is more a way of *being* than an isolated act of *doing*.

"Prayer is aimed at our deepest problem: our tendency to forget our connectedness with God. When this happens, we become lost in a sense of ultimate separateness. From this narrow outside-of-God place rise our worst fears, cravings, restlessness, and personal and social sinfulness."

Edwards describes two types of prayer. *Active prayer* is present where our wills shape our opening to God. Intercession, petition, confession, thanksgiving, and praise are forms of active prayer. These are forms of prayer that most of us learn as children and find reinforced in corporate worship and Scripture.

Quiet, contemplative prayer, he says, happens when we are still and open ourselves to Christ's Spirit working within us, when we heed the psalmist's plea: "Be still and know that I am God." (Psalms 46:10) We are in a state of quiet appreciation, simply hollowed out for God.

German theologian Meister Eckhart wrote:

"If the only prayer you say in your entire life is *thank you*, that will be enough."

Spiritual leader Marianne Williamson said:

"Prayer is when we talk to God. Meditation is when we listen."

In a book by the same name, author Anne Lamott wrote that there are three essential prayers:

"Help, Thanks, and Wow."

Thoughts On Churches and Rituals

Scholar Huston Smith wrote in The World's Religions:

"From a narrowly rational or utilitarian point of view, ritual is nonsense, a waste any way we look at it. All that money lavished on candles, cathedrals, prayer books, and incense; all the time spent in worship and sacrament; all the energy that goes into rising up and sitting down, kneeling and prostration, circumambulation and singing – to what end? ... Yet with all its arbitrariness and seeming waste, ritual plays a part in life that nothing else can fill, a part that is by no means confined to religion.

"Ritual eases us through tense situations and times of anxiety. Death is a glaring example. Ritual channels our actions and feelings when solitude would be unbearable. Ritual can smooth life's transitions, intensify experience and raise joy to celebration.

"Most simply, ritual can take something ordinary, like a blessing at a family meal, and make the occasion more than just the starting line for a food race. It can hallow the occasion and consecrate a daily pleasure."

Writer Norman Lear was quoted in The Wisdom of Sundays:

"I was walking with my friend Martin Marty, who was a great theologian at the University of Chicago. I asked him, 'Marty, what is the shortest description of worship you can give me?'

"He said, 'One word, Norman. Gratitude.' Worship is gratitude."

From The Color Purple, by Alice Walker:

"Have you ever found God in a church? I never did. I just found a bunch of people hoping for him to show. Any God I ever felt in church I brought in with me. And I think all the other folks did too. They come to church to share God, not find God."

"I think it pisses God off if you walk by the color purple in a field somewhere and don't notice it."

Other thoughts on going to church:

Joyce Meyer: "Just because you go to church doesn't mean you're a Christian. I can go sit in the garage all day and it doesn't make me a car."

Joshua Masters: "Do you want to be the church or just go to church? Because they're not the same thing."

Anonymous: "Church is not something you go to. It's a family you belong to."

Thoughts On Sin and Hell

Matthew 22:34-40:

"But when the Pharisees heard that he had silenced the Sadducees, they came together. And one of them, a lawyer, asked him a question, to test him. 'Teacher, which is the greatest commandment in the law?' And he said to him, 'You shall love the Lord your God with all your heart, and with all your soul, and with all your mind. This is the first and greatest commandment. And a second is like it, You shall love your neighbor as yourself. On these two commandments depend all the law and the prophets.'"

■■■

The Law of Karma:

Goodness is its own reward, and evil will always be its own punishment.

■■■

The late, great comedian, George Carlin, had lots of things to say about organized religion. Here's one tidbit:

"Religion has actually convinced people that there's an invisible man living in the sky who watches everything you do, every minute of every day. And the invisible man has a special list of ten things he does not want you to do. And if you do any of these ten things, he has a special place, full of fire and smoke and burning and torture and anguish, where he will send you to live and suffer and burn and choke and scream and cry forever and ever 'til the end of time!

"But He loves you. He loves you, and He needs money! He always needs money! He's all-powerful, all-perfect, all-knowing, and all-wise, somehow just can't handle money!"

■■■

In his books, The Universal Christ and The Spiral of Violence, Fr. Richard Rohr wrote about original goodness and sin:

"The true and essential work of all religion is to help us recognize and recover the divine image in everything. But in the fifth century C.E., Augustine first put forth the idea of Original Sin, which is not mentioned in the Bible at all. By contrast, most of the world's great religions start with some sense of primal goodness in their creation stories. Genesis tells us that God called creation "good" five times. The original metaphor was a garden. But after Augustine, most Christian theologies shifted from this positive view to a darker vision – the so-called fall. Instead of embracing God's master plan, Christians shrunk our image of both Jesus and Christ, and our 'Savior' became a mere Johnny-come-lately 'answer' to the problem of sin, a problem that we had largely created ourselves. That's a very limited role for Jesus. His death instead of his life was defined as saving us! This is no small point. Jesus became a mere mop-up exercise for sin, and sin management has dominated the entire religious story line and agenda to this day. This is no exaggeration.

"When we start with a theology of sin management administered by an elite clergy, we end up with a schizophrenic religion. We end up with a Jesus who was merciful while on earth, but who punishes in the next world.

"Instead, we need to find our Original Goodness, which we can discover when we own these three attitudes deeply planted within us:

- A trust in inner coherence itself. 'It all means something.' (Faith)
- A trust that this coherence is positive and going somewhere good. (Hope)
- A trust that this coherence includes me and even defines me. (Love)

"Usually, when negative energy is directed our way, we respond in kind, and give it back. But think of an electrical transformer that gets dangerous voltage in and turns it into usable power. That's what Jesus did – he did not return the negative energy directed at him – not during his life or on the cross. He held it inside and made it something better. That is how 'he took away the sin of the world.' He refused to pass it on. Until we all get that message, there will be no new world.

"In recent elections, you might have thought that homosexuality and abortion were the new litmus tests of authentic Christianity. Jesus was much more concerned about issues of pride, injustice, hypocrisy, blindness, and the pull of power, prestige, and possessions. We conveniently ignore this 95 percent of his teaching and focus on a morality that usually has to do with human embodiment, becoming righteous, judgmental, and upset about those pelvic issues. As Jesus put it in Matthew 23:23, 'You ignore the weightier matters of the law – justice, mercy, and good faith...and instead you strain out gnats and swallow camels.' We worry about what people are doing in bed much more than making sure everybody has a bed to begin with. Christianity will regain its moral authority when it starts emphasizing social sin in equal measure with individual (body-based) sin and weave them both into a seamless garment of love and truth.

"Hell is not what we've pictured it to be but simply a much-needed metaphor (found in most religions) for the ultimate tragedy of NOT choosing life and love."

Martin Luther King, Jr. said:

Perhaps the worst sin of life is knowing right and not doing it.

Chapter 7

How Do I Respond to "Circle of Life" Matters?

Birth, love, loss, aging, death, heartbreak, growing, declining, disappointment, tragedy. All are found in every life, and bad things <u>do</u> happen to good people.

When bad things happen, is it some kind of karmic punishment? Is it a lesson sent from God to teach me something? Or is it just something that happens and whatever meaning it has is what I make of it?

What do I need to remember as I navigate the hard times?

And the big question: What happens when I die?

Otherwise, by Jane Kenyon

I got out of bed
on two strong legs.
It might have been
otherwise. I ate
cereal, sweet
milk, ripe, flawless
peach. It might
have been otherwise.
I took the dog uphill
to the birch wood.
All morning I did
the work I love.

At noon I lay down
with my mate. It might
have been otherwise.
We ate dinner together
at a table with silver
candlesticks. It might
have been otherwise.
I slept in a bed
in a room with paintings
on the walls, and
planned another day
just like this day.
But one day, I know,
it will be otherwise.

This quote is from the movie, "The Best Exotic Marigold Hotel:"

"Everything will be all right in the end. So, if it isn't all right, it's not the end."

From a Center for Action and Contemplation Daily Meditation February 16, 2015:

"Human consciousness does not emerge at any depth except through struggling with your shadow. I wish someone had told me that when I was young. It is in facing your conflicts, criticisms, and contradictions that you grow up. You actually need to have some problems, enemies, and faults! You will remain largely unconscious as a human being until issues come into your life that you cannot fix or control and something challenges you at your present level of development, forcing you to expand and deepen. It is in the struggle with our shadow self, with failure, or with wounding, that we break into higher levels of consciousness. I doubt whether there is any other way."

In his book, Yes, And...., Richard Rohr wrote:

"We live in a finite world, where everything is dying, shedding its strength. This is hard to accept, and all our lives we look for exceptions to it.

"Suffering is the necessary *deep feeling* of the human situation. If we don't feel pain, suffering, human failure, and weakness, we stand antiseptically apart from it and remain numb and small. We can't fully understand such things by simply thinking about them.

"Pain teaches a most counterintuitive thing – that we must go down before we even know what up is. Suffering of some sort seems to be the only thing strong enough to destabilize our arrogance and our ignorance. I would define suffering very simply as whenever you are not in control.

"It eventually becomes evident that you're going to get nailed for any life of real depth or love. Some forms of suffering are necessary so that we can more fully know the human dilemma, so that we can even name our shadow self and confront it. Maybe evil itself has to be *felt* to understand its monstrosity and to empathize with its victims. We must all feel and know the immense pain of this global humanity. Then we are no longer isolated, but a true member of the universal Body of Christ. Then we know God not from the outside but from the inside.

"Love and suffering are part of most human lives. Without any doubt, *they are the primary spiritual teachers* more than any Bible, church, minister, sacrament, or theologian."

In "Fierce Love," Jacqui Lewis writes:

"Stay where the pain is. Right where you are, in the hurt and sorrow, that's right where the insight is, that's where the answer is, that's where the wisdom is. The transformation is there, the rebirth is there. And you're not alone. Your friend, your lover, your family, your helper – someone from your posse will midwife it with you. The healing will come, and you will emerge, shaped in the merciful womb of the fiercest love. The pain of birth is excruciating. But someone who loves you knows how to reach in and grab you and hold on to you until you make it through. You'll emerge lighter, less encumbered, ready for new stories, transformed by old ones."

Rumi wrote:

Inside the Great Mystery that is,
we don't really own anything.
What is this competition we feel then,
before we go, one at a time, through the same gate?

(Furuzanfar #1616)

Author and composer Paul Bowles said:

"Because we don't know when we will die, we get to think of life as an inexhaustible well. Yet everything happens only a certain number of times, and a very small number really.... How many more times will you watch the full moon rise? Perhaps twenty. And yet it all seems limitless."

Thoughts On Aging

In the chapter on aging, John O'Donohue wrote in his *book* *Anam Cara: Spiritual Wisdom from the Celtic World:*

"We have seasons of our life. When it is wintertime, you are going through pain, difficulty or turbulence. At that time it is wise to follow nature and withdraw into yourself. Nature's remedy is to hibernate and find sanctuary in the shelter of your own soul.

"Then we transition into springtime – a time of promise, hope and possibility. A time for making important changes, in the flow of your own growth and potential.

"Spring blossoms and grows into summertime – color, richness, and depth. You are in the flow of your own nature. You can take risks and land on your feet – a time of great balance.

"Summertime grows into autumn. The seeds sown in spring, nurtured by the summer, now yield their fruit. A time of harvest. Autumntime in a person's life can be a time of great gathering, harvesting the fruits of your experiences. Ageing is not merely about the body losing its poise, strength and self-trust. It is inviting you to become aware of the sacred circle that shelters your life and harvests your soul. Within your circle, you are able to gather your experiences, bring them together. As your body ages, you can become aware of how your soul enfolds and minds your body; the panic and fear of ageing falls away. When you begin to age, you see how quickly time is moving. The only difference between a young person at the height of their exuberance and a very old person at a very frail and empty physical level is time.

"Time passes and takes everything away. This can be consoling when you are suffering and going through a lonely, searing time. It is encouraging to be able to say: This too shall pass. The opposite is true when going through a lovely and happy time; you are with people you love and life could not be better. You secretly say to your heart: God, I wish this could continue forever! But it cannot; this too comes to an end. All of our time disappears on us.

"Old age, as the harvest of life, is a time where your memories and their fragments gather. You can appreciate them in a way you didn't when you were rushing through your days. You can forgive yourself. Heal your inner wounds. Accept that it is your life, and in everything negative that happened to you, there was always something bright hidden.

"Old age can be a time of freedom – freedom to let go of the false burdens we've been carrying around, many of which we've created for ourselves."

A Blessing for Old Age

May the light of your soul mind you,
May all of your worry and anxiousness about becoming old be transfigured,
May you be given wisdom for the eye of your soul,
To see this beautiful time of harvesting.
May you have the commitment to harvest your life,

To heal what has hurt you, to allow it to come closer to you and become one with you.
May you have great dignity, may you have a sense of how free you are,
And above all may you be given the wonderful gift of meeting the eternal light and beauty that is within you.
May you be blessed, and may you find a wonderful love in your self for your self.

From writer Joyce Carol Oates:

"I used to think getting old was about vanity – but actually it's about losing people you love. Getting wrinkles is trivial."

Thoughts on the Circle of Life

John O'Donohue also wrote:

"The Celtic world was always fascinated with circles, and they are prevalent in so much of its artwork. The eye finds deep consolation and sense of home in a circle – it satisfies some deep longing in us to belong 'inside the circle.' Earth is a circle. Embracing circles. Family circles. Stone circles. The Celts even transfigured the Cross by surrounding it with a circle. The circle around the beams of the Cross rescues the loneliness where the two lines of pain intersect; it seems to calm and console their forsaken linearity.

"The year is a circle. Winter gives way to spring; summer grown out of spring until, finally, the year completes itself in the autumn. The circle of time is never broken. Even the rhythm of the day is a circle – new dawn, strengthening towards noon, falling away towards evening, return of night. The life of each person is also a circle. We come out of the unknown. We appear on the earth, feed off the earth, and eventually return again to the unknown."

Black Elk, an Oglala holy man, said something similar (quoted by CAC):

"You have noticed that everything an Indian does is in a circle, and that is because the Power of the World always works in circles, and everything tries to be round. In the old days when we were a strong and happy people, all our power came to us from the sacred hoop of the nation, and so long as the hoop was unbroken, the people flourished. The flowering tree was the living center of the hoop, and the circle of the four quarters nourished it. The east gave peace and light, the south gave warmth, the west gave rain, and the north with its cold and mighty wind gave strength and endurance. This knowledge came to us from the outer world with our religion.

"Everything the Power of the World does is done in a circle. The sky is round, and I have heard that the earth is round like a ball, and so are all the stars. The wind, in its greatest power, whirls. Birds make their nests in circles, for theirs is the same religion as ours. The sun comes forth and goes down again in a circle. The moon does the same, and both are round. Even the seasons form a great circle in their changing, and always come back again to where they were. The life of a man is a circle from childhood to childhood, and so it is in everything where power moves. Our tepees were round like the nests of birds, and these were always set in a circle, the nation's hoop, a nest of many nests, where the Great Spirit meant for us to hatch our children.

"But the Wasichus [white men] have put us in these square boxes. Our power is gone and we are dying, for the power is not in us any more. You can look at our boys and see how it is with us. When we were living by the power of the circle in the way we should, boys were men at twelve or thirteen years. But now it takes them very much longer to mature.

"When we forget the roundness of life, the inter-being of all creatures and the Creator, we lose our sense of true identity and belonging – to that very circle."

In The Prophet, Kahlil Gibran wrote about Children, also reflecting the Circle of Life:

"And a woman who held a babe against her bosom said, Speak to us of Children.
And he said:
Your children are not your children.
They are the sons and daughters of Life's longing for itself.
They come through you but not from you,
And though they are with you yet they belong to you not.

You may give them your love but not your thoughts,
For they have their own thoughts.
You may house their bodies but not their souls,
For their souls dwell in the house of tomorrow, which you cannot visit, not even in your dreams.
You may strive to be like them, but seek not to make them like you.
For life goes not backward nor tarries with yesterday.

You are the bows from which your children as living arrows are sent forth.

The archer sees the mark upon the path of the infinite, and He bends you with His might that His arrows may go swift and far.
Let your bending in the archer's hand be for gladness;
For even as He loves the arrow that flies, so He loves also the bow that is stable."

Thoughts On Death and Dying

From writer Anne Lamott:

"You will lose someone you can't live without and your heart will be badly broken, and the bad news is that you never completely get over the loss of your beloved. But this is also the good news. They live forever in your broken heart that doesn't seal back up. And you come through. It's like having a broken leg that never heals perfectly – that still hurts when the weather gets cold, but you learn to dance with a limp."

Science fiction author Robert Heinlein:

"There is no conclusive evidence of life after death, but there is no evidence of any sort against it. Soon enough you will know, so why fret about it?"

Japanese writer Haruki Murakami:

"Death is not the opposite of life, but a part of it."

Richard Rohr:

"Being present at live birth and conscious death are probably the supreme catechism classes and Sunday schools that we have available to humanity. And yet we have turned them largely into medical events instead of the inherently spiritual events that they are."

In Anam Cara, John O'Donohue wrote on death:

"All fear is rooted in the fear of death. Life is uncertain and unpredictable. No one can say with certainty what is going to happen to us tonight, tomorrow, next week. Right now, things are happening to people all over the world that will change their lives forever. The only thing we can say with any certainty: a time will come, a morning, an evening or a night, when you will be called to make the journey out of this world, when you will have to die. You do not know where, how, when, who will be there, or how you will feel.

"For Celts, the eternal world was so close to the natural world that death was not seen as a terribly destructive or threatening event. When you enter the eternal world, you are going home to where no shadow, pain or darkness can ever touch you again.

"Death is a lonely visitor. When death visits your home, nothing is ever the same again. There is an empty place at the table; there is an absence in the house. Something breaks within you, which will never come together again.

"In the Celtic tradition there is a great sense that the dead do not live far away. There are always places where there is a memory of the people who have lived there. When a person is close to death, the veil between this world and the eternal world is very thin. Your friends, who now live in the eternal world, come to meet you, to bring you home.

"There is no need to be afraid. When the moment of your dying comes, you will be given everything that you need to make that journey in a graceful, elegant, and trusting way. If you live in this world with kindness, if you do not add to other people's burdens, but if you try to serve love, when the time comes for you to make the journey, you will receive a serenity, peace and a welcoming freedom that will enable you to go to the other world with great elegance, grace and acceptance.

"It is a privilege to be with someone who is making this journey into the eternal world. Be not so much concerned with your own grief as being fully present to, with and for the person making the journey, to make their transition as easy and comfortable as possible.

"Think of your death as an encounter with your deepest nature and most hidden self. It is a journey towards a new horizon. It is not a dark destructive monster that cuts off your life and drags you away to an unknown place. It is a release and invitation to freedom that can bring you to a completely new divine belonging.

"Death is not the end; it is a rebirth. The little band of brightness we call our life is poised between the darkness of two unknowns. There is the darkness of the unknown at our origin. We suddenly emerged from this unknown and the band of brightness called life began. Then there is the darkness when we disappear back into the unknown.

"The eternal world does not seem to be a place but rather a different state of being."

A Blessing for Death

I pray that you will have the blessing of being consoled and sure about your own death.
May you know in your soul that there is no need to be afraid.
When your time comes, may you be given every blessing and shelter that you need.
May there be a beautiful welcome for you in the home that you are going to,
You are not going somewhere strange. You are going back to the home that you never left.
May you have a wonderful urgency to live your life to the full.
May you live compassionately and creatively and transfigure everything that is negative within you and about you.
When you come to die may it be after a long life.
May you be peaceful and happy and in the presence of those who really care for you.
May your going be sheltered and your welcome assured.
May your soul smile in the embrace of your anam cara.

In his autobiography, "The Luckiest Boy in the World," Tim Quinn described a vivid dream he experienced of death:

"I remember that it was in the spring of the year during one of those first nights when you could have the windows open. Just before dawn I awoke to a cool breeze that carried the scent of lilacs. I then rolled over and fell into a deep, deep sleep. In that dream, death came to me peacefully and painlessly while I slept. There was an afterlife of consciousness, and it was the most peaceful and serene experience of my life. There was no pain and no worry. All of the things that I had worried about during my life were no longer important. I remember wanting to shout out to everyone that I knew and loved, 'Don't worry about it! It's all going to be OK! It really doesn't matter in the whole scheme of eternal life!'

"The dream ended, and I awoke, somewhat shaken by what I had experienced. At first, I tried to tell myself that it was just a dream. But it wasn't. Its impact would not be denied, and it didn't just go away. I can't say that I never worried again, but my approach to my life and my death definitely changed for the better as a result. It was one of a few of what I would call 'mystical' experiences that changed my world view forever."

Other Thoughts on Death and Dying

Rumi:

"Goodbyes are only for those who love with their eyes. Because for those who love with heart and soul, there is no such thing as separation."

English humorist Terry Pratchett:

"No one is actually dead until the ripples they cause in the world die away."

Bengali poet Rabindranath Tagore:

"Death is not extinguishing the light; it is only putting out the lamp because the dawn has come."

Henry David Thoreau:

"Live your life. Do your work. Then take your hat."

Winston Churchill:

"I am ready to meet my maker. Whether my Maker is prepared for the great ordeal of meeting me is another matter."

The truest words ever spoken, by Will Rogers:

"If there are no dogs in Heaven, then when I die I want to go where they went."

Thornton Wilder:

"The highest tribute to the dead is not grief but gratitude."

A final word from Maxime Lagacé, founder of WisdomQuotes:

"Do you see the gift that you had? Do you see how lucky you were?"

Chapter 8

What Other Thoughts Do I Need to Keep in Mind?

What are good things to remember as I go about living the rest of my life? What do I seem to need to be reminded of regularly? I've collected lots of little snippets of thoughts on life over the years. Each time I run across them in a drawer or tucked in a book, I think, "Yes!" They don't neatly fit into a category, other than "Random Stuff I Don't Want to Forget."

The Journey, *by Mary Oliver*

One day you finally knew
what you had to do, and began,
though the voices around you
kept shouting
their bad advice—
through the whole house
began to tremble
and you felt the old tug
at your ankles.
"Mend my life!"
each voice cried.
But you didn't stop.
You knew what you had to do,
though the wind pried
with its stiff fingers
at the very foundations,
though their melancholy
was terrible.
It was already late

enough, and a wild night,
and the road full of fallen
branches and stones.
But little by little,
as you left their voices behind,
the stars began to burn
trough the sheets of clouds,
and there was a new voice
which you slowly
recognized as your own,
that kept you company
as you strode deeper and deeper
into the world,
determined to do
the only thing you could do—
determined to save
the only live that you could save.

Author of Jonathan Livingston Seagull, Richard Bach:

"Here is the test to find whether your mission on Earth is finished: if you're alive, it isn't."

Author M. Scott Peck:

"All my life I used to wonder what I would become when I grew up. Then, about seven years ago, I realized that I was never going to grow up – that growing is an ever-ongoing process."

Indian-American author and alternative medicine advocate, Deepak Chopra:

"Think of your body as a *process* (not something finite.) You are constantly reinventing it. Things that help are sleep, meditation, movement, emotional well-being, a diet that is more plant-based and less processed. Wake up every day with the intention: I'm going to enjoy an energetic body and lightness of soul."

▪▪

Greek Stoic philosopher Epictetus:

"It's not what happens to you, but how you react to it that matters."

▪▪

Center for Action and Contemplation Daily Meditations 2/4/20:

Humans tend to live themselves into new ways of thinking more than think themselves into new ways of living.

▪▪

In The Prophet, Kahlil Gibran wrote:

"And an old priest said, Speak to us of Religion. And he said:

"Is not religion all deeds and all reflection? ... Who can separate his belief from his occupations? ... Your daily life is your temple and your religion. Whenever you enter into it take with you your all."

▪▪

Author Anne Lamott:

"I didn't need to understand the hypostatic unity of the Trinity; I just needed to turn my life over to whoever came up with redwood trees."

17th Century mathematician and philosopher Blaise Pascal:

"All man's miseries derive from not being able to sit quietly in a room alone."

Author Elizabeth Berg, in The Art of Mending, *talks about appreciating transcendent moments:*

"There are random moments – tossing a salad, coming up the driveway to the house, ironing the seams flat on a quilt square, standing at the kitchen window and looking out at the delphiniums, hearing a burst of laughter from one of my children's rooms – when I feel a wavelike rush of joy. This is my true religion: arbitrary moments of nearly painful happiness for a life I feel privileged to lead."

David Brooks wrote in his book, The Second Mountain*:*

"A commitment to faith is a commitment to stick with it through all the various seasons of faith and even those moments when faith is absent. To commit to faith is to commit to the long series of ups and downs, to intuitions, learning and forgetting, knowing one sort of God when you're twenty-five and a very different God at thirty-five, fifty-five, and seventy-five. It means riding out when life reveals itself in new ways and faith has to be reformulated once again. To commit to faith is to commit to change. It includes moments of despair, or it is not faith."

Quote often attributed to Michelle Ventor:

"People come into your life for a reason, a season or a lifetime. When you figure out which it is, you know exactly what to do."

American novelist Tom Robbins:

"The unhappy person resents it when you try to cheer him up, because that means he has to stop dwelling on himself and start paying attention to the universe. Unhappiness is the ultimate form of self-indulgence."

Anne Lamott:

I am all the ages I've ever been. Your inside person doesn't age. Your inside person is soul, is heart, in the eternal now, the ageless, the old, the young, all the ages you've ever been.

Journalist Jane Howard:

"Call it a clan, call it a network, call it a tribe, call it a family: Whatever you call it, whoever you are, you need one."

Benedictine sister Joan Chittister wrote of humanity's inherent attraction to both community and individuality:

"Life, we learn young, is one long, unending game of push and pull. One part of us pushes us always toward wholeness, toward a sense of connection with the universe which, in the very act of engagement with the human community, brings us a sense of peace. We are not here as isolates, we realize. We are here to become community.

"The other part of us, however, pulls us back into ourselves. It separates us from the universe around us and leaves us feeling distant and out of sync. We lack the sense of kinship that the human family is a family. We say we seek unity, yes. But lurking within every human act is the gnawing need to be independent.

"It is this paradox of life that stretches us not only to grow but to contribute to the growth of the rest of the universe around us.

"Thomas Merton also recognized this same paradox. The best way to love ourselves is to love others, yet we cannot love others unless we love ourselves since it is written, 'Thou shalt love thy neighbor as thyself' [Mark 12:31]. But if we love ourselves in the wrong way, we become incapable of loving anybody else.

"Only when we see ourselves in our true human context will we begin to understand the positive importance not only of the successes but of the failures and accidents in our lives. My successes are not my own. The way to them was prepared by others. The fruit of my labors is not my own: for I am preparing the way for the achievements of another."

Zen philosophy:

Infinite gratitude...to all things past.
Infinite service...to all things present.
Infinite responsibility...to all things future.

Hebrew prophet Micah: "O human being, this is what God desires for you. That you do justice. That you love kindness. That you walk humbly in the presence of your God" (Micah 6:8).

Brian McLaren wrote about this stating that Micah turns a religious question into a human question. He said Christians very much like to call Jesus the *Son of God.* Jesus much preferred to call himself the *Son of Man* (or *son of humanity*). There are many layers of meaning to the term. But the simplest and most obvious is this: a *son of humanity* is a *human being.* If you want to put a finer point on it, *son of* means *the essence of* or perhaps *a new generation of.* Jesus is saying that he represents the essence of humanity, a new generation of humanity, a new kind of human being. In this light, his constant invitation, *follow me,* means *imitate me* and *join me on my journey toward a new way of being human*.

McLaren stated:

> "In that light, whatever you choose to call yourself, Christian or not, I hope you will aspire to be a *humble* human being . . . *religiously.*
>
> "I hope you will desire to be a *kind* human being, because that person you call your enemy is part of your family, part of your species, part of your story, part of your kind.
>
> "And in addition to being a humble and kind human being, I hope you will aspire to being a *just* human being. Don't seek power over others to control or exploit them or harm them. Instead, use whatever power that comes your way for the common good, so that all people everywhere can share equal justice and equal dignity. Seek justice. Love justice. Do justice. Be a just human being . . . *religiously.*
>
> "When I say *religiously,* I mean *intentionally,* seeking out practices that promote justice, kindness, and humility. And I mean *collaboratively,* joining or building communities or networks that promote those practices. And I mean *reverently,* knowing how precious this heartbeat and this breath really are, and feeling every moment how much danger and opportunity are held in these human hands. R*eligiously,* as I'm using the term, means *with a sense of the sacredness of everything* and a commitment to re-consecrate everything."

Anne Lamott:

"I'm here to be me, which is taking a great deal longer than I had hoped."

Lyrics from "The Impossible Dream," written by Joe Darion:

To dream the impossible dream
To fight the unbeatable foe
To bear with unbearable sorrow
And to run where the brave dare not go

To right the unrightable wrong
And to love pure and chaste from afar
To try when your arms are too weary
To reach the unreachable star!

Margaret Wheatley wrote in *<u>Leadership and the New Science</u>:*

"Fractals are a scientific phenomenon. What appears to be chaos actually happens within a boundary. A shape appears over time, so that what appeared to be random was actually within the pattern and each small piece is a smaller version of the whole. This applies to organizations. The best ones have a fractal quality – any observer can tell by watching anyone what the organization's values and ways of doing business are. We can use our own lives as evidence for this because they evolve in just such a fashion. By the end of our lifetime, we are able to discern our individual basins of attraction. What has been the shape of our life? What has made seemingly random events now appear purposeful? What has made 'chance' meetings fit smoothly into the movement of our lives? We discover that we have been influenced by a meaning that is wholly and uniquely our own. We experience a deeper knowledge of the purpose that structured all of our activities, many times invisibly and without our awareness. Whether we believe that we create the meaning in a retrospective attempt to make sense of our lives, or that we discover meaning as the preexistent creation of a purposeful universe, it is, at the end, only *meaning* that we seek. Nothing else is attractive, nothing else has the power to cohere an entire lifetime of activity."

Richard Rohr:

"God is both utterly beyond me and yet totally within me at the same time."

From Deepak Chopra, <u>The Book of Secrets: Unlocking the Hidden Dimensions of Your Life:</u>

"If you obsess over whether you are making the right decision, you are basically assuming that the universe will reward you for one thing and punish you for another.

"The universe has no fixed agenda. Once you make any decision, it works around that decision. There is no right or wrong, only a series of possibilities that shift with each thought, feeling, and action that you experience.

"If this sounds too mystical, refer again to the body. Every significant vital sign—body temperature, heart rate, oxygen consumption, hormone level, brain activity, and so on- alters the moment you decide to do anything... decisions are signals telling your body, mind, and environment to move in a certain direction.

"No single decision you ever made has led in a straight line to where you find yourself now. You peeked down some roads and took a few steps before turning back. You followed some roads that came to a dead end and others that got lost at too many intersections. Ultimately, all roads are connected to all other roads."

The Three Goals, by American poet David Budbill

The first goal is to see the thing itself
in and for itself, to see it simply and clearly
for what it is.
          No symbolism, please.

The second goal is to see each individual thing
as unified, as one, with all the other
then thousand things.
          In this regard, a little wine helps a lot.

The third goal is to grasp the first and the second goals,
to see the universal and the particular,
simultaneously.
          Regarding this one, call me when you get it.

Bishop T.D. Jakes:

"Stop watering things that were never meant to grow in your life. Water what works, what's good, what's right. Stop playing around with those dead bones and stuff you can't fix, it's over...leave it alone! You're coming into a season of greatness. If you water what's alive and divine, you will see harvest like you've never seen before. Stop wasting water on dead issues, dead relationships, dead people, a dead past. No matter how much you water concrete, you can't grow a garden."

Richard Rohr:
"So where is God revealing God's self? Certainly not in the 'safe' world, but at the edge, at the bottom, among those people and places where we don't want to find God, where we don't look for God, where we don't expect God. The way we've shaped Christianity, one would think it was all about being nice and middle class and 'normal' and under the law. In the Gospels, Jesus, Mary, and Joseph are none of those things, so they might just be telling us we should be looking elsewhere for our status and dignity. Maybe the reason that our knowledge of God is so limited is because we've been looking for God in places we consider nice and pretty. Instead, God chooses the ordinary and messy."

A Blessing of Solitude, *by John O'Donohue*:

May you recognize in your life the presence, power and light of your soul.
May you realize that you are never alone, that your soul in its brightness and belonging connects you intimately with the rhythm of the universe.
May you have respect for your own individuality and difference.
May you realize that the shape of your soul is unique,
That you have a special destiny here
That behind the façade of your life there is something beautiful, good and eternal happening.
May you learn to see your self with the same delight, pride and expectation with which God sees you in every moment.

Chapter 9

What is My Credo?

"First say what you would be; and then do what you have to do."

- *Epictetus*

After collecting all these various thoughts, reflecting, sorting, and winnowing out what feels true, two big questions remain – What do I, personally, believe? And then, given what I believe, how should I live my life?

Almost 25 years ago, I participated in a study/discussion group that culminated in each person writing their own Credo statement. The word "Credo" comes from the Latin word meaning "I believe." It is a statement of the beliefs or aims which guide someone's actions.

Key parts of a credo include:

1. Who am I?
2. What do I believe? What beliefs govern my life?
3. What is my purpose? What are the desired results of my life?
4. Therefore, what do I need to do? How should I live?

A credo should be a living document, one that is revisited on a regular basis and revised as you learn more, experience more, and grow in your understanding of your own particular life's patterns.

I encourage you to draft your own statement. It can be in any format that makes sense to you, as long as the above questions are answered. Before putting together this book, I had not updated mine in 25 years, so it was way past time. As an example, here is today's version of my Credo.

Credo

I believe….

- …there is a God. To me, God is the all-encompassing wisdom, love, and creative energy in the universe, all that is Good. God is what holds the universe together – from stars in the sky to every cell in our body. I do not believe God is an old man in white flowing robes, sitting on a throne in puffy white clouds, passing out judgement, and keeping a naughty/nice list like a vindictive Santa Claus. God is neither He nor She; God just is.

- …Heaven and Hell are consequences of behavior experienced here on earth when we are either connected to or disconnected from that love. "Going to heaven" and "going to hell" are not physical places we go when we die; rather, they are metaphors for the positive and negative results of our actions or inactions.

- …in Original Goodness. Every person (and every creature) is born of God and made from creation's Original Goodness. As life goes on, people may learn to hate, may make unfortunate decisions based in ignorance or fear, or are hurt, causing them to behave in ways that are non-loving. This makes them hard to love, but they are also God's creatures and need to be loved.

- …there is one main commandment – to love my neighbor as myself and to do unto others as I would have done to myself. I need to hold myself to that standard and not blindly accept any other edicts of manmade "sins." I believe there are loving and unloving thoughts and actions, and I will experience the corresponding consequences. I don't believe we are "forgiven for our sins" or that "Jesus died to save me from my sins." I need to work to atone my own behavior.

- ...I am a Christian, because I cannot say that I am not. I believe that Jesus' purpose was to show us how we human beings can and should live. I believe in the messages he shared and the example he provided. I feel most like a "Celtic Christian," because I find my spirit so much in nature and in those spiritual beliefs. I reject any form of Christianity that doesn't focus on living the loving message of Jesus or that uses the faith label as a weapon against others.

- ...that the Bible teaches many wonderful lessons about life and our spirit. Many of these lessons are story examples or metaphors, and not necessarily the literal truth. Because the Bible has been compiled, translated, and modified over centuries by multiple humans with varying motives and levels of enlightenment, I do not believe that every word or verse of the Bible can stand on its own as the absolute truth. If a passage passes the litmus test of "loving your neighbor," it probably is true and good.

- ...prayer connects us with the universal spirit. It is good to connect to that spirit to give thanks for this wonderful life, to express awe in creation, or to tap into when trouble is encountered and strength is needed. I don't believe that the universe is organized around making me happy, nor does God plan little surprises for me to cope with. Things happen, and I can learn from them and take meaning from them. But

I also believe it is helpful to connect with the ultimate positive energy source for strength when life's challenges come my way.

- ...when I die, my spirit will return to the great source of energy and love. I probably won't look like myself, may not even be "myself," and for sure won't be sitting around chatting with angels in a permanent state of bliss. But I trust and have faith that it will all be good. I'll greet other spirits (human and animal) I have loved and who have loved me. I don't understand what stroke of luck caused my spirit to come down and be born to my particular set of parents in the Midwest in the 1950's. I just appreciate how lucky I have been and know that it will all continue to be well with my soul.

Because I believe those things, I need to live my life as follows, to the best of my ability:

- I need to have respect for all creation and not intentionally harm. This means:
    - Respecting myself and my body, taking good care of what I've been given.
    - Respecting other people, being kind, understanding, and not being hurtful, in spite of how others may act; trying to truly love my neighbor as myself.
    - Respecting nature and the world, trying to live and work in a manner that doesn't destroy God's creation.
- I need to appreciate my gifts, resources, and talents and use them to help others. This means:
    - Being thankful and living with gratitude; connecting with my spirit each day.

- Being a good steward of what I have been given; being responsible for myself and not dependent on others; continuing to grow and learn.
- Being generous with my talents and resources to help make life better for others; continuing to identify specific ways I can contribute (in even small ways) to improving life for others.

If I do those things, when my life is over, I'll be at peace and have no regrets.

Bibliography

Following are the books and sources mentioned most often in the prior chapters, plus a few extras that have provided meaningful perspectives but may not have been quoted.

Anam Cara: Spiritual Wisdom from the Celtic World, John O'Donohue, Bantam Books, 1997.

The Center for Action and Contemplation online resources, www.cac.org.

Complete Poems of Robert Frost, Holt, Rinehart & Winston, 1964.

The Color Purple, Alice Walker, Pocket Books, 1987.

Conversations with God: An Uncommon Dialogue, Neal Donald Walsh, GP Putnam's Sons, 1995.

Do I Stay Christian: A Guide for the Doubters, the Disappointed, and the Disillusioned, Brian McClaren, St. Martin's Essentials, 2022.

Good Poems for Hard Times, selected by Garrison Keillor, Penguin Books, 2005.

Help, Thanks, Wow: The Three Essential Prayers, (and any of her other books) Anne Lamott, RiverHead Books, 2012.

In Search of Stones: A Pilgrimage of Faith, Reason, and Discovery, M. Scott Peck, M.D., Hyperion, 1995.

Leadership and the New Science: Discovering Order in a Chaotic World, Margaret Wheatley, Barrett-Koehler Publishers, 2001.

Long Walk to Freedom: The Autobiography of Nelson Mandela, Back Bay Books, 1995.

A Prayer for Owen Meany, John Irving, William Morrow & Co., 1989.

The Prophet, Kahlil Gibran, Alfred A. Knopf Inc., 1923.

The Rumi Collection, Shamhala Classics, 2000.

The Second Mountain: The Quest for a Moral Life, David Brooks, Random House, 2019.

The Servant as Leader, Robert Greenleaf, The Greenleaf Center for Servant Leadership, 1973.

The Seven Spiritual Laws of Success: A Practical Guide to the Fulfillment of Your Dreams, Deepak Chopra, AmberAlen, 2007.

Super Soul Sunday broadcast series on OWN
www.oprah.com/app/super-soul-sunday

Teaching with Fire: Poetry that Sustains the Courage to Teach, Jossey-Bass, 2003.

The Wisdom of Faith with Huston Smith, Bill Moyers, PBS special series, 1996.

The Wisdom of Sundays: Life-Changing Insights from Super Soul Conversations, Oprah Winfrey, FlatIron Books, 2017.

The World's Religions, Huston Smith, HarperSanFrancisco, 1991.

The Universal Christ: How a Forgotten Reality Can Change Everything We See, Hope For, and Believe, Richard Rohr, Convergent, 2019.

Yes, And.... Daily Meditations, Richard Rohr, Franciscan Media, 1997.

Cover Photo: Taken by the author at a ruin in the Scottish Highlands, 2018.

About the Authors

Michelle (Shelley) Keith is retired and following the sunshine between Northern Michigan and Southern Florida. She was the co-founder and former vice president of the Michigan Leadership Institute and was engaged by The Eli and Edythe Broad Foundation to partner on creation and management of the Broad Superintendent's Academy. Prior to that, she had 20 years of higher education experience in the areas of human resources, planning and governance at Northwestern Michigan College and Iowa State University, where she earned a bachelor's and master's degree. Michelle is married to Tim Quinn and is the proud grandma of five fabulous grandchildren.

Tim Quinn has served at all levels of public education leadership, from K-12 through community college and university. He was superintendent of the Green Bay Public Schools, president of Northwestern Michigan College, and chief executive officer of Michigan's first virtual college. Tim was the founder and former president of the Michigan Leadership Institute and was engaged by The Eli and Edythe Broad Foundation to partner on the creation and management of The Broad Center and Broad Superintendents Academy. He earned a Ph.D. from The University of Michigan and received honorary doctoral degrees for statewide leadership in education. Tim is the proud father of two education administrators and grandfather of a quintet of gifted grandchildren.

www.ingramcontent.com/pod-product-compliance
Lightning Source LLC
LaVergne TN
LVHW012111160826
845678LV00014B/3047

* 9 7 9 8 3 5 3 8 3 3 9 8 7 *